ON THE DUTY OF CHRISTIAN CIVIL DISOBEDIENCE

WRITTEN BY

PETER DEMOS

FIVE
STONE
PRESS

Romulus, Michigan

On the Christian Duty for Civil Disobedience
by Peter Demos

ISBN 978-0-9988171-7-0

For Worldwide Distribution, Printed in the U.S.A.

FiveStonePress
Every Book a Giant-Killer
An imprint of Supernatural Truth Productions, LLC
www.FiveStonePress.com

Acknowledgments

To not start off acknowledging God—the Father, Son, and Holy Spirit—as my primary Source of inspiration and guidance would be wrong. God has been so good to me, saving me from a path of ultimate destruction, and has given me strength, comfort, and peace during the times I am fearful and desperate. The perfect logic of His Word has made writing this book much easier than I thought it would be at the start.

Kristin, my wife, has been amazing through the process. She is such a kind soul who has to handle any backlash that I may receive for our beliefs and for my mouth. In *Afraid to Trust*, her chapter she wrote—"Jealous of Jesus"—is a glimpse of what she has to tolerate from me; but she has been so strong and keeps me focused on things when I want to run all around.

Kristin and my children have helped me so much in the writing of this book as well. It was our conversations during the 2020 pandemic lockdown, or when we were working side by side trying to keep our restaurants working, that inspired me to ask, "What do we do if . . . ," and helped me find the answers in the Bible.

My pastors at World Outreach Church, Allen Jackson and Malcolm Hedding, along with Pastor Shane Ogle at Great Lakes Church in Troy, Michigan, have been so inspirational to me in their patience— allowing me to ask tough questions and engage in discussions of right and wrong during times such as these.

Hanna Edington, my ghost-writer, has been amazing to work with. At times, it felt like she was sharing my brain, and I would watch her write words that somehow captured not only my thoughts but my pattern of speech as well.

I want to acknowledge those politicians, pastors, and media personalities—some of which I know personally and others I know from watching the events around the world—who have allowed corruption to enter their hearts. Seems odd to acknowledge them, but they truly were a source of inspiration as I had to determine how to respond to them in a godly way and not in a worldly way (which I wanted to do).

Lastly, there are so many others whom I have left out but are part of this process, including you who read this book. You are not forgotten or unappreciated, but I cannot allow my acknowledgments to be greater than the substance, so I must stop here.

With love and peace,

Peter Demos

Table of Contents

Introduction

THIS WASN'T THE BOOK I PLANNED TO WRITE THIS YEAR. I HAD something on my heart that I was looking forward to diving into, but as I looked at what was happening around me, I felt moved to go in a different direction.

Not only was 2020 a year of major upheaval for most people, but it also seemed to be a time when things started to get uncomfortably real. All of the warning signs that Christianity might not be welcome in this country for much longer seemed to be growing more and more potent.

While we do still maintain many of our freedoms in comparison to some other parts of the world, we must prepare for the times to come. The Bible warns us that a day will come when the wheat and the chaff will be separated and we have to be prepared in advance, knowing how we will respond when it grows difficult to live out our faith in public.

Further, it won't be obvious to us as this separation takes place. In Matthew 24:37–39 and Luke 17:28–30, Jesus tells us that at the end of time, people will be carrying on in their normal lives, eating and drinking, and engaging in business. In other words, evil will slowly take over our lives. Even as our day-to-day activities continue, we will be caught off guard if we are not watchful.

With that in mind, we have to ask the question: Why now?

Over the past few years, we have seen a major shift in legal cases brought against Christians throughout America and other western or 'secular' societies. The courts are increasingly siding with those who view Christian practices as discriminatory or unjust.

Likewise, through the sudden appearance of COVID-19, one of the most unprecedented aspects we saw was the government responses against businesses and religious institutions.

While many have argued that churches have not been persecuted during this time because *everything* was being shut down equally, there has been a very strange perspective on what exactly is considered essential. Although we will look at this more in-depth later on, it is curious to note that strip clubs, liquor stores, protests, and casinos have been essential while many churches and small businesses have not. Further, many church leaders have also voluntarily given up their essential status under the guise of "loving others".

However, the author of Hebrews tells us in 10:24-25, "And let us consider how to stir up one another to love and good works, not neglecting to meet together, as is the habit of some, but encouraging one another, and all the more as you see the Day drawing near."

While it is important to look at verses like this in their whole context, this chapter is relating to Christ's sacrifice for us as well as the full assurance of our faith.

How is our faith acted out in response to His sacrifice? How do we respond when we are told to forsake the assembling together in the church? And while no one knows the day or the hour when Jesus will return, that Day is *always* drawing nearer. Although no one knows when the end of times is coming, we do know that as you read this, it is closer than it was yesterday and tomorrow it will be closer than today.

In modern times, Christians are very good in our use of *Christianese* and our claim to orthodoxy. What we miss—and what our ancestors tended to boast much stronger—is the reality of our faith.

What does faith look like when we are in the midst of even the most subtle persecution? And what does it look like when those subtleties begin to compound and strengthen?

We have a perfect opportunity right now to decide how we will respond as the grip tightens and as the world tells us more and more than our beliefs are not in line with acceptable thought. Our faith has an opportunity to shine, but not without consequences.

In Matthew 28:19-20, the Great Commission states, "Go therefore and make disciples of all nations, baptizing them in the name of the Father and of the Son and of the Holy Spirit, teaching them to observe all that I have commanded you. And behold, I am with you always, to the end of the age."

There are no provisions in this for succumbing to laws, regulations, and popular thought. This is our act of faith and this is what must be carried out even in the midst of attack. As believers in Jesus, we must be ready to fear God[1] more than we fear man.

The speed of COVID-19 caught us off guard, and we reacted to it the best way we knew how. I had mistakenly criticized leaders while defending myself from others from criticizing my leadership. In reality, we were all in the same boat, caught up in a massive storm—watching the water pour in unprepared and praying for the best.

If we all had considered this possibility and prepared for such an event, we likely would have been in better shape. Therefore, we, as Christians, need to be prepared for what is next when it comes to our potential loss of freedom of the worship of our Christ.

As I have seen shifts in culture toward hostility and shifts in the church toward submission, my heart has grieved. For that reason, I want to encourage you to be ready and to know exactly what you are standing for and why it is important.

We have a great opportunity now to stand in spite of culture and honor God through obedience to His Word. If that does not fall in line with the authorities, we have a choice to make.

The time to choose is now.

---

[1] *Fear* in reference to God is often used as a sign of 'awe' or 'respect' as opposed to 'terror'

CHAPTER 1:

Why is This Important?

THE PAINFUL REALITY IN THE WORLD TODAY IS THAT CHRISTIANS ARE under attack. Indeed, Christians have always been under attack, from the Roman lion pits to the underground churches in China. It's nothing new.

What *is* new is that Christians in America are facing persecution in a way that we haven't ever before.

Some of these things are obvious. For instance, we have seen how prayer in public schools has been removed. Not only that, but it has been criticized and is now greatly frowned upon being considered an affront to inclusion and deeply offensive to many.

The understanding of 'everyone has the right and freedom to worship as they wish'[2] has shifted toward 'I have the right and freedom to not see how you worship and if I see it, you are infringing

---

[2] See <u>Reynolds v. US 98 US 145 (1878)</u>: George Reynolds, secretary to Brigham Young, was charged with bigamy. The US Supreme Court unanimously ruled that belief in polygamy was fine, but you could not act on it any more than if your religious belief included human sacrifice or bride burning.

on my own rights'. This change in our understanding has led to a surprising and dramatic belief that the freedoms we possess only belong to us if others keep their own freedoms out of our faces.

Many cultural Christians have adopted this model, giving credence to this view by not speaking up in the public square and remaining silent as attacks on the Church has slowly escalated.

As Christians, our mandate to go into all the world and preach the Gospel lives in direct contradiction to that understanding.

But prayer in public schools is hardly the only area in which we have seen the obvious attacks against Christianity. In the responses to the COVID-19 pandemic, churches appeared to be at the top of the list for shutdowns.

While many have claimed that this cannot be considered persecution because *everyone* and *everything* had to shut down, the facts do not reflect this as strip clubs, liquor stores, abortion clinics, and casinos have been able to remain open. It really is remarkable how innovative some churches were in being allowed to remain open.

For instance, two churches in San Diego, California rebranded themselves as 'family friendly' strip clubs in order to remain open.[3] Why? Because, according to a court order, strip clubs are considered a constitutional right and should not have to be shut down in the midst of a pandemic.[4]

---

[3] Soulpurposemag.com 2020-11-24, & Soulpurposemag.com. (n.d.). Strip clubs essential, NOT churches so San DIEGO Church calls itself 'FAMILY friendly Strip club'. Retrieved April 10, 2021, from https://www.newsbreak.com/news/2108323918043/strip-clubs-essential-not-churches-so-san-diego-church-calls-itself-family-friendly-strip-club
[4] By removing his tie, the pastor claimed he was "stripping"

But these two churches were not the only ones who got creative during this season.

We have seen churches fight for the freedoms extended to protests, which are considered a right undeterred by lockdowns. Others have declared themselves to be casinos so that they might be afforded the luxury of being 'essential' during this time, and in Pennsylvania, one church held service in a Wal-Mart.[5]

However, this season in America's history opened the eyes of many to the reality that Christians were promised. Although we have not been forced underground and we have not been thrown into pits with the lions, it has been a season in which we can meditate on the words of Jesus in John 15:18-25,

> "If the world hates you, know that it has hated me before it hated you. If you were of the world, the world would love you as its own; but because you are not of the world, but I chose you out of the world, therefore the world hates you. Remember the word that I said to you: 'A servant is not greater than his master.' If they persecuted me, they will also persecute you. If they kept my word, they will also keep yours. But all these things they will do to you on account of my name, because they do not know him who sent me. If I had not come and spoken to them, they would not have been guilty of sin, but now they have no excuse for their sin. Whoever

---

[5] Geller Report by Pamela Gellar August 10, 2020

hates me hates my Father also. If I had not done among them the works that no one else did, they would not be guilty of sin, but now they have seen and hated both me and my Father. But the word that is written in their Law must be fulfilled: 'They hated me without a cause.'"

We are not greater than our Master, and if they hate Him, they will hate us as well. Bearing that in mind, we can accept that these measures which, on the surface appear that they are for the right cause—stopping the spread of a highly contagious illness—are actually far more complex.

The world may hate Christ, but it loves the things of the flesh. It would not be popular in the news to share the disparity between shutting down churches and keeping strip clubs open, but it is easy for those who set their minds on the things of the flesh[6] to believe that this is a crucial right, whereas church is an outdated Sunday ritual that we won't miss.

There are those who may believe this is simply an oversight—that out of a desire to protect the people in this country, churches were closed and the phases of reopening happened to favor other establishments instead. But is that really the case? Have the multitude of inconsistencies and even court cases not shown that there is an intention behind it all?

Observing the variations between what is and is not considered essential is deeply worrying. But there are also a number of ways,

---

[6] Romans 8:5

prior to the COVID-19 pandemic in which the attack on Christians is less obvious, and that is something we need to be even more concerned about. The enemy we see isn't half so worrisome as the one we cannot see.

So what are some things that have been subtle?

The first one is the Affordable Care Act.

Regardless of a person's political views on the advantages or disadvantages of this institution, there is one thing which stands as a stark offense against Christians in America today.

Birth control.

But is it really birth control? That is what it has been simplified to. When Hobby Lobby refused to provide their employees with access to abortive medications through their healthcare, headlines raged about their denial of *birth control* for employees.[7]

In reality, Hobby Lobby was refusing a small number of select pills which could be used for abortive purposes. There were still many pregnancy-prevention pills they were willing to provide to employees through their healthcare.

But this raised a question regarding how far the government could go in controlling both businesses and Christians. Just what were they allowed to do? What demands could they make on businesses when those demands went against the Christian consciences of the business owners?

---

[7] "It's Not Just Hobby Lobby: These 71 Companies Don't Want To Cover Your Birth Control Either." Jaeah Lee *Mother Jones* 2 April 2014; "Justices Rule for Hobby Lobby on Contraception Mandate" Richard Wolf *USA Today* 3 July 2014; "The 82 Employers who want to deny Birth Control Coverage" Miriam Berg *Planned Parenthood Blog* 18 July 2014

And how much farther have those demands come in the days since?

Beyond this, we have also seen an increase in the rights of Christians being stripped when it comes to matters of the LGBTQ[8] community.

There was a time in America's history when people could disagree with one another and still get along. Two people from different walks of life could have a heated debate and then go fishing together. Unfortunately, this has changed. Instead of being allowed to disagree with our friends, family, and neighbors, we have been told that if we do not support someone's choices, we must hate them.[9]

For Christians who stand in strong defense of traditional Biblical principles, the push for LGBTQ inclusion has presented a very challenging problem.

While we absolutely are called to love others, Christians are also called to hate sin. We are called to hate our own sin and, yes, to hate sin in others. It has never mattered who has the sin, but sin itself is to be detested.

So when we declare that any sexuality aside from the marriage of one XY male and one XX female is sin, we are saying that it must be hated.

---

[8] I have seen these acronym for to be as large as LGBTQIA+ and LGGBDTTTIQQAAPP. For simplification purposes, I have limited this label to LGBTQ. As a firm believer in asking people what language they prefer, I have discussed with multiple friends and acquaintances who are members of this community how many letters ought to be included in the label and the consensus has been to simplify it to these five.

[9] I recently ran across a cartoon during the 2020 election that read, "Guess who will still be your friend no matter who you vote for…. Not me, because I am not friends with Communists"

Of course, what seems to be misunderstood these days is how easy it is to hate someone's sin while still loving and caring for that person. But because the Christian view of same sex attraction and other matters of gender and orientation is viewed as a direct attack, there has been an intense attack in return.

This has been further exacerbated as Christians have remained silent on other sexual sins like pornography, prostitution, and adultery. These glaring silences, combined with the intensity against the LGBTQ community, feels more personal to those in that community.

It is unfortunate that we see so many disappointing things from the Church that end up in the public eye.

On one hand, we see sheer hatred from people like the infamous Westboro Baptist Church who represents such an extremist view that there is none of God's grace to be found. Sadly, much of the United States looks at this church as the prime example of how deeply Christians hate the LGBTQ community.

However, there is also a strong movement in the church for acceptance and even praise of those who are members of this community. Many churches declare that it is not an issue of sin, and it is not an affront to the Lord but rather something placed in the Bible due to some cultural context.

There are also those who believe that it is an error in translation. For these apologists, the belief is that the Biblical use of the word for 'homosexuality' was actually a reference to pedophilia or rape.

Prominent Christian figures[10] have made these declarations, and now these sects of the church are seen as acceptable to the world. While translation theory—such as the fact that the Bible has been translated into more than 1,300 languages, and in every language this has been the accepted meaning of the word—is easily proven wrong as ancient translations are shockingly accurate, we are seeing that the church has begun to bow to culture in agonizing droves.

We Cannot Keep Silent

As believers in Christ, we must decide whom we fear more—God or the world. And if our answer is to fear the Lord as the Bible tells us, we have to be firm and unashamed of the beliefs we hold.

This will be frightening at times, and it may lead us into places we don't want to go, but we have the choice to make. Will we bow or will we be like Shadrach, Meshach, and Abednego? Will we stand firm before the flames?

An important note that we have to acknowledge is that *God does not need us to defend Him.*

He is God. He holds the entirety of the world in His hands, and He has no need for our pitiful praise. He will be glorified whether we give Him the glory or not. Just as Jesus tells us in Luke 19, even if we do not praise the Lord, the rocks will cry out.

---

[10] https://www.facebook.com/jenhatmaker/posts/friends-brandon-wrote-a-longer-explanation-of-our-process-if-this-might-be-helpf/1084514128314248/

AN ARGUMENT AGAINST THE USE OF THE WORD 'HOMOSEXUAL' IN ENGLISH TRANSLATIONS OF THE BIBLE. Richie, C (2010)
https://onlinelibrary.wiley.com/doi/abs/10.1111/j.1468-2265.2009.00496.x
-"How the Bible became Anti-Gay: Forging a Sacred Weapon,
http://canyonwalkerconnections.com/forging-a-sacred-weapon-how-the-bible-became-anti-gay/

The simple existence of creation is honoring and glorifying to God. Each snowflake is a wonder of the works of His hands, and every morning when the sun rises, it is a sign of His order in creation.

So as we remember that this is the God we are striving to honor, we must remember that our praise of Him and our steadfastness in living for Him are not favors we must do for God. He has never *needed* us.

And if we acknowledge this truth, we have to ask why we bother then. If we are not honoring Him for His own sake and he doesn't need our defense, why should we defend Him?

The Bible is quite clear in the Great Commission that we are meant to go and make disciples. Further, faith comes by hearing and through those that verbalize the Gospel, as we are reminded in Romans 10:14-17. This world is lost. In our human eyes, we may see that it is deeply unfair that some of us have the gift of redemption while others do not; but what good is our redemption if we do not act as vessels who proclaim the truth to those who are lost?

The importance cannot be overstated. It is significant for us to use our knowledge of the Lord's goodness for the sake of others. We are meant to share with them—to show them just how deep the love of God is.

A part of this love is also God's inherent demand for justice. This justice requires that the wages of sin must be paid—which they have been through Christ. But the covering of Christ comes through repentance. Played out, our obedience to the Great Commission is also seen through our ability to share the truth that sin must have its reckoning.

As we speak the truth and proclaim it to those who are lost, we have to share with them the importance of repentance even when that is not popular. We live in a postmodern world where truth is considered relative to any distinct person.

To call something sin when a person identifies with that sin is not popular, but it is the truth under which we live. As believers that there is one truth and one law under Jesus, there is little choice for us aside from sharing that.

Silence is not the answer when the truth of the Bible and the law of God are under attack. There are a significant number of examples in Scripture to show us just how important this is.

We serve a God who knows us. He knows our hearts, and He knows the hearts of those who have not chosen to seek Him in return.

Unashamed

Romans 1:16 is a challenge to us when it says, "For I am not ashamed of the gospel, for it is the power of God for salvation to everyone who believes, to the Jew first and also to the Greek." And when we read this, we must ask ourselves if we live accordingly.

As believers are faced with the challenge of refusing to stay silent, we understand that God is the one who has the power for salvation. We are vessels, but we are not the ones capable of changing hearts.

God's chosen people was once exclusively Israel, but now, salvation has been bought once for all. When we see a weakened Christianity on display, the power of God's holiness is not lessened in actuality, but it is diminished in the human view. We lose the awe factor when we make God a mere extension of ourselves instead of seeing Him as the righteous judge and creator of the universe that He truly is.[11]

What unbeliever would devote their life to a God who is created in our image? How could they be swayed by His demand for justice, when His idea of justice is nothing more than 'your truth is my truth'?

To quote the apostle Paul, by no means! This is not the God we serve. The only god for us to be ashamed of is the god of our own making. Our idols are shameful, but the holy God is not. As we are faced with trial, tribulation, punishment, and further consequences we will look at later, we can ask ourselves if the God we are worshiping is worth the cost.

Furthermore, to keep silent from speaking about God will create stress in your life. Even David, in trying not to sin with his tongue, suffered the consequences for it in Psalm 39:1-5.

If the answer is no, God is not worth these consequences, it may be time for a reevaluation of who we believe God to be.

---

[11] 1 Corinthians 4:20 and 1 Thessalonians 1:5

What the Bible has to Say about Cowards

Unfortunately, there have always been cowards, even in the Church. Throughout history, we have seen so many men abuse the name of Christianity by using it for their own means and purposes, but one of the ugliest things we have seen is when leaders have behaved as cowards.

There have been celebrity pastors frightened by the world and too ashamed to call abortion a sin. There have been prominent Christians on social media and with their own reality television shows who regard homosexuality as a cultural issue and not a sin issue.

What does the Bible say about those who stand behind the Book but tear out the pages they dislike?

It says they are cowards.

The book of Revelation is frequently noted as being rather apocalyptic. No matter where the world is at in the last days, whether we are nearing Christ's return or whether we have a million years to go, there are some striking comparisons between what we see in Revelation and what we see in the world today.

"But as for the cowardly, the faithless, the detestable, as for murderers, the sexually immoral, sorcerers, idolaters, and all liars, their portion will be in the lake that burns with fire and sulfur, which is the second death."[12]

This is the second to last chapter in the Bible and it is the last verse before John tells us of his visions of the New Jerusalem. It is a warning that just as the faithful are on the cusp of eternity in the bliss

---

[12] Revelation 21:8

of God's presence, those who are faithless will be cast away from the presence of the Lord forever.

Let our warning be this: it is not only those who deny God who are cowardly. There are also a great many who proclaim to be His servants who have abandoned the orthodoxy of the Bible and have fled to their own desire for a truth that converges with popular society and what is considered acceptable in the modern world.

It is terribly distressing to think how many of our brothers and sisters have abandoned truth for the sake of *love* and *acceptance*. It is distressing to acknowledge that in the name of loving our neighbor as ourselves and in the name of grace, many have decided that it can only be right that we accept and praise those who are living in sin because it is who God created them to be. Or that for the sake of preventing the suffering of unwanted children, it is better that women have the option of terminating those children they are unable to care for.

These are not examples of love. The same loving Jesus who suffered not only the pain of the cross, but the pain of separation from His Father, of whom He is a part, was also the Jesus who turned over tables in the temple. He is the same Jesus who rejected sin and declared it, publicly shaming the self-righteous and privately confronting the tenderhearted.

He is the same Jesus who, when discussing sexual sin, revolutionized the idea that sexual sin began in the mind, long before it could ever be acted out. The loving Jesus who is full of grace and mercy also set a higher standard for what Israel believed to be holiness.

Derek Prince reminds us that some Christians confuse "God is love" with its inverse: "Love is God." Further, love that separates people from God and produces disobedience to His Word is illegitimate love.[13]

In light of this, we have to know that we are absolutely sinners and we will absolutely fall short from time to time. But to deny that our sin is an affront to God makes us cowards.

In Matthew 25, we read the Parable of the Talents. It is not a palatable parable in our modern times, but it does outline how we are to live and what we are to do with what we have been given. It begins by saying, "For it will be like a man going on a journey, who called his servants and entrusted to them his property."

Certainly, we have been entrusted with salvation. Salvation belongs to our God, first and foremost, but He has given it to us freely, just as the master has given to his bondservants. But the parable goes on...

> "To one he gave five talents, to another two, to another one, to each according to his ability. Then he went away. He who had received the five talents went at once and traded with them, and he made five talents more. So also he who had the two talents made two talents more.

---

[13] Prince, Derek *Protection from Deception* Whitaker House 2008 p 82

"But he who had received the one talent went and dug in the ground and hid his master's money. Now after a long time the master of those servants came and settled accounts with them. And he who had received the five talents came forward, bringing five talents more, saying, 'Master, you delivered to me five talents; here, I have made five talents more.' His master said to him, 'Well done, good and faithful servant. You have been faithful over a little; I will set you over much. Enter into the joy of your master.'

"And he also who had the two talents came forward, saying, 'Master, you delivered to me two talents; here, I have made two talents more.' His master said to him, 'Well done, good and faithful servant. You have been faithful over a little; I will set you over much. Enter into the joy of your master.'

"He also who had received the one talent came forward, saying, 'Master, I knew you to be a hard man, reaping where you did not sow, and gathering where you scattered no seed, so I was afraid, and I went and hid your talent in the ground. Here, you have what is yours.' But his master answered him, 'You wicked and slothful servant! You knew that I reap where I have not sown and gather where I scattered no seed? Then you ought to have invested my money with the bankers, and at my coming I should have received what was my own with interest.

"So take the talent from him and give it to him who has the ten talents. For to everyone who has will more be given, and he will have an abundance. But from the one who has not, even what he has will be taken away. And cast the worthless servant into the outer darkness. In that place there will be weeping and gnashing of teeth."[14]

What are we to do with the grace we have received? Are we to multiply it? Are we to go out into the world and share it with others so that our Master draws in the souls of the lost? Or are we to hide our faith like cowards? Are we to be so frightened that we will anger the Lord by doing things the wrong way that we disregard the Great Commission that He has mandated for us?

The coward, in this parable, is cast away. In fact, Jesus calls this man "wicked", a moniker that Jesus used rarely to describe people who were not Pharisees. Because he was afraid to use his gift from the Lord wisely, he is stripped of it and thrown into the outer darkness.

This parable in Matthew 25 comes directly after the Parable of the Ten Virgins and right before a series of verses about the Final Judgment. Because reading the Bible in its whole context is crucial to understanding it, we can see that this parable is absolutely referring to

---

[14] Matthew 25:14–30, ESV

how we are to live as Christians and how our obedience to the Lord will be reflected in the end.

What Shall We Say?

There is much to fear in this world and as Christians in America are faced with increasing odds against us, we do have to think about our response to those who come against us. We have to be prepared, but we must be also prepared to keep our perspective and our response in line with the Bible.

No matter what threats come against us when we are under attack, we know that the things of this world are temporary. We are not promised an easy life, according to the Bible. We are not promised health and wealth, we are not promised popularity or promotions.

But we are promised that nothing will separate us from the love of God in Christ Jesus our Lord.

Romans chapter 8 is one of the most quoted, meaty parts of the Bible that we can instantly recognize. Pastors preach it constantly, some Bible schools require students to memorize it for graduation, and songs have been written based on selections of it.

But one verse must be considered when we look at our role as Christians in the world in a time or circumstance of persecution on any level:

> "What then shall we say to these things? If God is for us, who can be against us?"

This verse, Romans 8:31, asks two deeply important questions.

What then shall we say to these things? What will you say to these things? How will you respond when you are faced with loss of friends or family, loss of status or privilege, loss of circumstances to the point that you cannot even feed your family or they are in danger because of your devotion to Jesus?

We all have to consider it as the day draws nearer and nearer. Jesus says in Luke 14:26, "If anyone comes to me and does not hate his own father and mother and wife and children and brothers and sisters, yes, and even his own life, he cannot be my disciple."

Does this mean that we are meant to hate those who God has put in our lives? Absolutely not! But it does mean that our devotion to Him must be paramount. It means that even when the most important people in the world to us are at stake—whether they deny us because of our faith or we are persecuted to the point of their lives being in danger—we must always choose obedience to Jesus.

So what shall we say? We must decide to live in accordance to His Word and say that we have been saved by grace through faith from the evils of our own sin and that others may join us by taking up their cross, denying their sin, and following Jesus.

But what about the other question in this verse from Romans 8?

If God is for us, who can be against us?

As it happens, there are many who can be against us. There just aren't any who matter.

If God is for us, if He is truly on our side as we believe Him to be, does it really matter that our boss fires us for praying in the lunch room? Does it matter that we are stormed by police for worshipping when worship is outlawed? Does it matter when we are declared hateful by the media because we praise the way God has genetically coded us, fearfully and wonderfully?

Does it even matter when our own father or wife or child denies us because of our passion for truth?

I certainly don't mean to diminish the pain of any of that. Putting our families in danger for our love of the Lord is an excruciating thought. For those mothers who live in nations where Christianity is outlawed, the knowledge that their children's lives are in danger must be agony. Likewise, even when persecution in the US was pitifully small, it was still painful.

Whether a Federal Appeals Court declares it unconstitutional to include *under God* in the Pledge of Allegiance,[15] or a governor is openly mandating that church attendees are not allowed to sing in their services, or a nation declares Christianity a death sentence, it is always difficult to hear.[16] [17]

And that is how it *should* be. While the small things are not an offense against us, every minimal persecution should grieve us because it is an affront against God.

As an American, I should not be offended when the Pledge of Allegiance is reworded.[18] But as a Christian, I must grieve the

[15] Nieves, E. (2002, June 27). Judges ban pledge of allegiance from schools, citing 'under god'. Retrieved April 10, 2021, from https://www.nytimes.com/2002/06/27/us/judges-ban-pledge-of-allegiance-from-schools-citing-under-god.html

[16] Meeks, Alexander "With a worsening Pandemic, California bans singing in places of worship." CNN.com 3 July 2020

[17] "Being a Christian is a death sentence" The Washington Times online 22 December 2001

[18] Elk Grove Unified School District v. Newdow; Jane Doe v. Acton-Boxborough Regional School District

knowledge that God's name has been declared too controversial and too undesirable to be honored. Again, He will still be glorified whether every American or no American acknowledges Him, but our chief end is to glorify God and to enjoy Him forever. Therefore, when He is being forgotten or banished from the things of this world, we have to continue in our declarations of His deity.

And those who do not?

They are the cowards that we read about. They are the ones who offer excuses and who have bowed to what the world wants and declares to be important, going so far as to deny the truths that Jesus declared.

Whoever is Ashamed of Me

There are consequences of every action, including those which come as an affront to the Lord. When we hide out and live according the patterns of the world, Jesus declares the consequences of that in Luke 9:26 when He says, "For whoever is ashamed of me and of my words, of him will the Son of Man be ashamed when he comes in his glory and the glory of the Father and of the holy angels."

Sometimes churches will put this as simply, "If you deny Me, I'll deny you." Although this is painful to accept, the reality is that our devotion to Jesus must be far above our devotion to the things of this world, so much that we refuse to be cowards even in the face of extreme persecution.

There have been many who have come before us who have done just that. The examples in the chapters to come look at believers in

God who took a stand for His Name's sake, as well as looking at those who chose civil disobedience for the sake of morality, even when their own lives did not reflect a belief in the God of the Bible.

But as Christians, our disobedience to the things of the world must always be in line with honoring God. Our motivation should consistently be in favor of loving Him first.

When we read this verse from Luke, it is easy to get caught up in the fear of it. After all, we should absolutely be frightened by the idea that Jesus may deny us. However, this fear should also be out of love for Him.

Just as our motivation to obedience should be our love of God as opposed to the idea of Heaven, our fear of the Lord must be greater than our fear of Hell. Heaven and Hell are endpoints, but what they represent is far greater.

Will we spend eternity *in* the presence of God or *without* the presence of God?

Our lives in this world must reflect that we are unashamed. As we proclaim the truth of His goodness and His grace and love for us, we have to likewise proclaim that a life lived in denial of God will lead to an eternity outside of His presence.

That eternity is one of terror, and the driving force is a love of sin.

A Final Look

Bringing all of this back, let's look once more at why it is important we examine this topic now.

Christians are under attack. The attack is through slander from the world, spewing hatred and claiming that we are the ones who have been unloving because of our devotion to truth. The attack is through defamation of the Name of the Lord. The attack is through the lot of the world. The attack is to deny that we are special in God's eyes.

But the attack is also through the cowardice of many who claim to be Christians. It is through those who are frightened by the world and think they can serve two masters, simultaneously declaring themselves to be followers of Jesus as they refuse to see the betrayal of sin against Him.

So when we have the obvious attacks against the church from the outside world, plus the less obvious attacks against truth from within by those who claim to be members of the Body of Christ, we cannot keep silent. We have to stand firmly against these attacks and continue pushing for boldness.

When we are shamed by the world for our obedience to Jesus, we make John 15:18–19 our mantle when He said, "If the world hates you, know that it has hated me before it hated you. If you were of the world, the world would love you as its own; but because you are not of the world, but I chose you out of the world, therefore the world hates you."

God gives us the strength to be hated, and we can endure all for the sake of His Name.[19] Regardless of what the world says, we are to speak out and proclaim the truth to the lost. If we do not, we are

---

[19] 2 Peter 1:3

rejecting what gifts God has given us and allowing ourselves to be like the lazy bondservant.

Let us instead be bold.

CHAPTER 2:

Answering through Civil Disobedience

THROUGHOUT HISTORY, CIVIL DISOBEDIENCE HAS BEEN USED AS A means of peacefully expressing disagreement with the laws of those who rule or govern. It is a nonviolent, peaceful method of protesting regulations and restrictions that are unethical or immoral.[20]

Although there are many famous examples of what this looks like, the term became famous in modern history by Henry David Thoreau, who wrote a book on it. In addition to his many activist beliefs—as well as those which drifted toward anarchism—he once spent a night in jail for refusing to pay his poll taxes.[21]

Thoreau was not simply refusing to pay his taxes because he wanted to get out of it and keep the money for himself. Rather, he was frustrated by the thought that this money could be used to

---

[20] There are countless examples of Civil Disobedience throughout history, and it would be impossible to cover them all with sufficient detail. I encourage you to read and learn about each of the historical examples I give below.
[21] Thoreau, Henry David *Walden or, Life in the Woods and On the Duty of Civil Disobedience* Supplementary Material written by Alyssa Harad. Pocket Books 2004 XIV and XV

support the Mexican-American war, with which he strongly disagreed.

Although some of Henry David Thoreau's beliefs did agree that violence was, at times, justified, he never acted it out in his own life. He chose to display pacifistic means of mutiny rather than violently fighting against the things in which he did not believe.

Joh Rawls has argued that Thoreau was advocating conscientious refusal as opposed to Civil Disobedience.[22] Rawls theorizes that civil disobedience should be limited to a political act and guided by political principles in order to change the law or politics of government.[23] Rawls further states, "Our natural duty to uphold just institutions binds us to comply with unjust laws and policies, or at least not to oppose them by illegal means as long as they do not exceed certain limits of injustice. Being required to support a just constitution, we must go long with one of its essential principles, that of majority rule."[24]

Martin Luther was not trying to engage in a political act when he engaged in a civil disobedience that ultimately led to the Protestant Reformation.

During the time of extreme corruption and disobedience by the ruling Catholic Church, Martin Luther, a Catholic monk, visited Rome. After seeing the corruption, he determined that faith—and not monetary payments—would lead to the forgiveness of sin.[25]

---

[22] Rawls, John "Theory of Justice" Belknap Press of Harvard University Press 1971 p 368
[23] Ibid p 364
[24] Ibid p 353
[25] Mataxas, Eric *Martin Luther: The man who rediscovered God and Changed the World* Penguin Books 2018 p 87-88

When Martin Luther rose up against the Catholic Church and the Papacy who were then living in extreme disobedience to the Lord, he risked himself for a principle. He posted 95 theses on the church door, recognizing that as a believer in Christ, his choice to live according to the Bible could result in excommunication from the Church.

Luther was faced with threats from every side. He understood that he could lose everything—and he lost much. On top of the external conflicts of losing friends, having his name slandered, and essentially tearing apart the accepted brand of Christianity that had been corrupting the church for years, Luther lost his peace. He suffered through extreme depression from the pressure, as well as guilt for the violence that had been undertaken by offshoots of his peaceful Protestantism.

Still, Luther held to his beliefs, aware that there could be great consequences for himself. Excommunication from the church and the possibility of prison or assassination were constant threats against him.

Nevertheless, he persisted. He did not stop with his 95 theses but wrote many more articles about the Word of God in the face of the ruling authorities of the day.[26]

Luther serves as a great reminder to us as to the distinct roles of church and state. When we look at Pope Leo X and his relationship with the Holy Roman Emperor Charles V (the two of whom banded together to have Luther excommunicated and declared a heretic and

---

[26] Metaxas p 229-231

outlaw), we can see that church and state cannot be the driving forces of one another. Both are subject to the law of God, and when there is extensive corruption taking place against that law, we have no choice but to stand, we cannot do otherwise.[27]

And if we move from Martin Luther to another well-known figure in civil disobedience, we find Mahatma Gandhi, whose hunger strike was both peaceful and effective in expressing his anger against British tyranny in India.

Gandhi's view of civil disobedience was that it was meant for the purpose of changing the hearts of one's opponents or the public. It was not allowed to be hostile in actions or words, and neither was secrecy permitted. His view of Civil Disobedience was that one should refuse to cooperate with his opponent.[28]

In addition to Gandhi's fasting, he engaged in a march of protest, known as the Salt March, joined by thousands of Indians, covering roughly 241 miles of land. This march was a response to the British tax laws on salt and how they refused to give the Indian people the freedom to source it on their own.

In an act of Civil Disobedience, Gandhi began to walk, addressing people in villages as he passed through them and encouraging them to join him. They walked until they reached the coastline of the Arabian Sea where he began to harvest salt from the sand.[29]

---

[27] For example, see Luther's famous quote from the Diet of Worms: "I neither can nor will retract anything; for it cannot be either safe or honest for a Christian to speak against his conscience. Here I stand; I cannot do otherwise; God help me! Amen."

[28] Shephard Mark "Mahatma Gandhi and His Myths, Simple Productions 2011 p 24

[29] Sinha Sarojii *A pinch of Salt Rocks An Empire* Prabhat Prakashan 2015 pp24-26

The consequences were numerous and resulted in some 80,000 people arrested in the following weeks, plus significant numbers of police beatings and Gandhi's eventual arrest. But even Winston Churchill declared these protests a great humiliation for Britain, and their impact is still widely seen in modern times. Ultimately, Gandhi's non-violent civil disobedience toppled the largest empire at that time and brought about India's sovereignty as a nation. There is no denying that Gandhi's actions made their mark on the world.

A man inspired by Gandhi and frequently confused with the Reformer, Martin Luther King Jr., is another prime example of Civil Disobedience.[30] Honestly, the list of examples are extensive, but a few highlights of his activism are the Montgomery Bus Boycott—in which he led a boycott against the company following Rosa Parks's civil disobedience, refusing to give up her seat for a white man—and the March on Washington to demand an end to segregation, in which he delivered his famous *I Have a Dream* speech.

MLK, a Christian pastor, obviously influenced by Christian values and beliefs, did see Civil Disobedience as the ability to gain the attention necessary to draw lawmakers into negotiations to make the civil change. King—like Rawls, Luther, and Ghandi—believed in non-violence but felt that the purpose of the non-violence was to end in a negotiation.[31]

Regardless of religious beliefs and motivations, Civil Disobedience has been used throughout history to incite change.

---

[30] Kumar Priyanka "What King Learned from Gandhi" Los Angeles Review of Books 16 January 2017
[31] Morris, Lisa Anne "What Martin Luther King said about Civil Disobedience" Medium 3 August 2014

These four examples are hardly exclusive, but they do give us insight into the methods that have been used, as well as some of the consequences (such as imprisonment and assassination) that can come from engaging in these activities. Nevertheless, when something is worth fighting for, we have to fight.

The Christian's Test for Civil Disobedience

Although I have long relied on the works and examples of these men (and many other courageous men and women throughout Biblical and modern history), they are still flawed when considering each one as a Christian.

Christian civil disobedience transcends political civil disobedience. Christians serve a Kingdom that is outside the realm of politics and recognizes that justice, outside of a Biblical framework, is inherently unjust. As St. Aquinas and St. Augustus agreed, an unjust law is no law. Although our response may be to political or legal pressures, it can also be a response to cultural pressures.

As believers in Christ, we are under a microscope. These days, that microscope might look like a Facebook algorithm that determines whether or not our beliefs constitute as hate speech.

Since becoming a Christian, I have been told how I am supposed to act by people of faith, including what I call "fire-fighting Christians" (legalist Christians who like to "put the fire out"). But I have also been told how I am meant to act by non-Christians, including Wiccans and Satanists. People want to analyze and determine if a Christ-follower must be like a socialist who gives all of the hardworking tax-payer's money away to social programs in order to love our neighbor. Or they may say Christ-followers are only those who fight for the pre-born while banishing the alien and stranger among us.

Regardless, as Jesus told us in the Gospels, following Jesus has been politicized, polarized, and analyzed into something rather different from marvelous salvation "by grace through faith."

And as the world watches what we do and how we do it, we have a simple question to ask in every action and reaction. This question is imperative before we embark on any journey of Civil Disobedience.

Does this 100% comply with the words of Jesus and the Bible as a whole?

While this is a question we would all do well to ask more often, when it comes to standing firmly against culture, government, and even the progressive church, we must remember that there are eyes on us at all sides. So how are we going to respond? Will we take up arms? Will we do battle through bloodshed? Through refusal to pay taxes? Through starvation?

There are methods extreme and simple, violent and non-violent, loud or quiet. Many methods are devoid of sin and simply come down to where the Lord is leading you. For instance, we may believe that starving ourselves is harming the body God has given us, but Christians have always been called to fast. Will our fasts be God-honoring? Or will they reflect the Pharisees who went about in sackcloth in ashes, expressing their deep suffering and hunger for attention?[32]

Likewise, are we engaging Civil Disobedience for a *reason* that complies with the words of Jesus and the Bible as a whole?

This is where we have to ask ourselves if we are simply unhappy with a decision being made by the ruling authorities or if it is truly a situation in which we are forced to participate—actively or passively—in a crime against the law of the Lord.

It is certainly easy to find laws we disagree with or dislike. But are they truly against God? Does our choice to stand against them comply with what we have been taught by Jesus?

The Bible does make it clear that God appoints leaders—for better, for worse, and for a reason. We are also told to give to Caesar what is Caesar's.

When we are angry that our taxes are going toward abortion facilities, we can easily stand firm in defiance and shout that it would cause us to actively participate in sin. But when Jesus said those words to His people in Matthew 22, He was speaking to a people who were paying taxes to a corrupt leadership who treated them poorly. There were no provisions for avoiding sin by avoiding taxes. Instead, we have been directly told to live under the authority of the land.

This is part of the difference between being in the world and not of it. We do still have to live our lives here. We do have to be subject to ruling authorities. The difference is that we are subject to the law

---

[32] Matthew 6:16

of God above those authorities and we can only stand against our worldly rulers if we must to be completely obedient to Jesus.

Theologies may vary on the level to which the Holy Spirit speaks to us, but we have to be cautious as to whether we are led by the Holy Spirit or by our own desires, which we can easily project as being the words of Jesus. Therefore, we also have to consider if our choice for Civil Disobedience is in line with the nature of the Bible.

The Bible is where we find incidents like Jesus turning over tables in the Temple, Esther fasting as she silently worked for the freedom of her people, and David cutting the garment of King Saul, sparing his life to not harm him.[33]

How do these incidents compare? Was Jesus justified in defying those who were turning the temple of God into a place where riches were reaped? Absolutely! It was a defilement of the place where the Spirit was meant to dwell. Jesus saw how God's glory was being cheapened or ignored, and He could not abide such an act.

What about Esther as she wooed her husband—an evil king— through her grace and pure heart while striving to undo a terrible law that was put forth by a narcissist to destroy God's chosen people? Certainly, Esther was able to continue worshiping her Creator while effecting change. She maintained her obedience to God while undermining one of the most important men in Israel.

And then, there is David. There are few men in the Bible portrayed with so many dimensions as David, and that is one of the reasons why this incident is so striking.

---

[33] David spared Saul's life one more time when Saul was sleeping but took his spear and water jug instead in 1 Samuel 26.

While hiding in a cave from Saul (who was trying to kill him), David cut a corner of cloth from Saul's clothing[34] and then retreated.

Why would he do this? Why would David bother risking the chance that Saul might catch him and kill him there? Or why wouldn't he just go ahead and kill Saul first, before Saul had a chance to strike?

One school of thought is that David simply wanted to send a warning to Saul while another said that by taking the hem of the garment, he was symbolically transferring the kingdom from Saul to David. Regardless, David, twice, wanted to let Saul know that he had been close enough that he *could* have killed him, but he didn't. Essentially, David wanted Saul to be afraid.

Ultimately, however, after the first time, when Saul had a lucid conversation with David, guilt got a hold of David, and he could no longer allow himself to get away with this clever little warning.

He realized that he had disobeyed God through this silent activism because he had made an effort to harm the Lord's anointed. It may not have been a physical or detrimental harm, but Saul was certainly showing that his thoughts were fractured enough without David giving him more reason to jump at shadows or worry about losing his Kingdom

As we seek to prepare for a time in which we may have to engage in Civil Disobedience, we have to ensure that our actions are in line with the nature of the Bible, that we are showing the due respect that

[34] 1 Samuel 24

we have been told to show those who rule over us, but ultimately reserving the highest honor of obedience to God above all else.

And this is when we can engage in disobedience while still being obedient to God. If our methods are honoring to God, showing a righteous anger against what dishonors Him (as opposed to a childish anger that makes our own betterment the primary goal), we can still live in obedience to Him.

As French theologian John Calvin stated, "A dog barks when his master is attacked. I would be a coward if I saw that God's truth is attacked and yet would remain silent."[35]

Our Master is worthy of more than cowardice. In Him, we find the strength to bark.

The Christian Duty and Nonviolence

On its own, Civil Disobedience can absolutely be violent or nonviolent (even though Rawls would argue that it cannot be[36]). There are many options. However, our Christian duty will always naturally lead us to nonviolence.

We will look at examples in the following chapter, but the importance of nonviolence cannot be overstated.

There are many who argue that the God of the Old Testament was perfectly pro-violence. Just look at how many wars He led Israel into! However, when we look at those examples, we do see a lot of extenuating circumstances.

---

[35] "A Dog Barks" Return to Truth, Exhorting Godliness, 13 September 2017 accessed 8 March 2021
[36] Rawls, p366

At various points, we see other nations in the land that God had designated for Israel; we see them coming to attack God's chosen people; and we see Israel acting out of God's jealousy for His own glory.[37] These were times when the battles belonged to the Lord, and they were fought for His name.

Contrast this with incidents such as the Crusades, when the battles for religious sites were generally fought with hatred, brutality, and for purposes of political gain. It was generally less about preserving the name of God and more about expanding an empire.

For us, as individuals, our Christian duty leads us to nonviolence. There is no option in which our lashing out in violent protest is going to glorify God. Rather than inspiring those against us to turn to God, they will become victims of the Christian tyranny that they already believe we display through our moral viewpoints.

As we engage in Civil Disobedience, it is extremely important for us to bear in mind that our actions must always be carried out only for the sake of honoring the Lord. Anything less is driven by sin and our own pride.

Throughout 2020, the choice that many churches made to continue worshiping regardless of government mandates was Civil Disobedience. For some churches who were allowed to continue worshiping together, they engaged in Civil Disobedience by choosing to sing in church when it was forbidden.

---

[37] This phrase can make us uncomfortable, but when we think of God in context of who He is, there is nothing arrogant about His desire to be worshiped. Every god in every culture desires the worship of their followers. It is the very nature of a "god" to be the object of worship.

Unfortunately, Christianity has been directly called out in reference to the January 6, 2021 riots that took place at Capitol Hill. Reports from The Atlantic, NPR, and The New Republic all suggest that Christianity was responsible for the violence that took place that day, while many others infer a link to Christian nationalism.[38] It really is appalling that something so vicious and irresponsible could be cited as an act of our faith.

But when we look at the events leading up to that day, we see that these protestors—certainly not acting out of any true faith in Christ—were acting out of fear for what they believed the next administration would take from them or do to the nation. They were also acting in response to the 2020 Black Lives Matter protests that shook the nation and likewise led to many deaths.

The Black Lives Matter protests took place out of fear and anger after yet another black man was killed by police in an unjust manner. Although there were many peaceful protests, even in my hometown of Murfreesboro, Tennessee, the news reported many others that resulted in violence, looting, and fires across the nation. The death of

---

[38] Green, E. (2021, January 08). A Christian Insurrection. Retrieved April 10, 2021, from https://www.theatlantic.com/politics/archive/2021/01/evangelicals-catholics-jericho-march-capitol/617591/

Gjelten, T. (2021, January 19). Militant Christian Nationalists remain a potent force, even after the Capitol riot. Retrieved April 10, 2021, from https://www.npr.org/2021/01/19/958159202/militant-christian-nationalists-remain-a-potent-force

Sutton, M. (2021, January 14). The Capitol Riot revealed the darkest nightmares of White Evangelical America. Retrieved April 10, 2021, from https://newrepublic.com/article/160922/capitol-riot-revealed-darkest-nightmares-white-evangelical-america

George Floyd was a catalyst for a new wave of protests that got out of hand.

But why are we seeing such ugly cause and effect?

Violence may work, but the problem is that with violence comes destruction of property, the environment, and sometimes life. When this happens, your opponents can point to your bad acts as a justification for not changing. The important thing to remember is that civil disobedience is meant to cause a change of heart. Even if you cannot change their heart, you can keep them from finding fault in what you do. The last thing we want—and what we see happening—is that people are simply going underground with their hate and/or anger even though it may not appear so from a cursory view.

Non-Violence is not passive. It is aggressive. And as we will see in Chapter 10, the purpose will result in violence toward us in response to the aggressive nature of non-violence.

A Story

Imagine a beautiful black-tie affair at a stunning event center in Middle Tennessee. Men left their honey-do lists at home, skipping college football, or cutting their golf games short so they could spend a good hour getting into their tuxedos and gelling their hair into obedience. Women, now clad in beautiful gowns and sporting their favorite shades of lipstick, were smiling as if they hadn't just rushed a dinner for their kids and broken up several fights over who should have control of the remote. Everyone was schmoozing, politely asking about each other's work and families while supporting (some altruistically and others selfishly) the wonderful charity that was hosting the event.

After dinner and a few speeches, the music started, and about half the guests got up to dance. A few people took this as their cue to leave, while others sought out the faces of those we knew for some friendly conversation.

I have to admit, I wasn't really in the mood for this kind of party that night. I can't dance, and loud music makes it hard for me to hear conversations. It was a long day at the end of an even longer week. I was tired and grumpy, but my wife does enjoy dancing, and she can hear people for the conversations. Since we don't go to many of these events, we were going to stay.

Quite a few friends were hanging out by the music, but I can't hear well in loud environments, and I tend to come across as rude when I don't mean to be, so I left the main hall and found some friendly faces near the bar. Some were only casual acquaintances of mine, but several I knew quite well.

I realized as we talked that many of them were no longer sober. As they chatted about local affairs, their tongues were looser than they might otherwise have been, and I found myself becoming increasingly uncomfortable. I couldn't really point my finger on any one thing that was said that caused me such discomfort, but there were subtle undertones. A certain level of ego was present, evidenced in the ways they talked about anyone who didn't quite fit into the same peer group. It reminded me of movies where the men who ran the cities sat around smoking cigars, drinking brandy, and plotting their next move. Criticism about "other" groups seemed a little harsher than necessary; ethnic groups referred to as "they" and "them" in a tone that hinted at disapproval. Subtle mockery of Christianity began, even by men who claimed to be Christians themselves. In truth, these men were behaving in the exact same way I once had not so long ago, before God confronted me in a radical way.

I wasn't in a position to judge them—even if I could from a worldly perspective, I certainly couldn't from a Christian one. God knows all of things that I have done before I was saved and the things I have failed at after I was saved. I certainly couldn't look at someone and say they are or they are not Christians. Truthfully, my mood and attitude did not reflect a Christian heart, and anyone observing me that night from the outside looking in could have concluded I wasn't a Christian either.

Many of them were churchgoing men. Their children went to private schools—which in Tennessee tend to be Christian leaning. And, like I said, nothing they said or did was overtly sinful (save, of course, the drunkenness). I may not have even noticed it if I had been in a different sort of mood that night. But perhaps because I wasn't keen to be there and had found myself on the outside of the circle, I was a little more critical than usual. I couldn't help but wonder how the conversation would look to a total outsider.

When I practiced law, I always was shocked at reading the transcripts of court cases and depositions as they did not reflect tone, butchered dry humor, and never reflected context. I am certain you have experienced this with text messages and emails as well. So I recognized that if anyone read the transcript of the conversation, it would have sounded much worse that what they were meaning

I went home that night feeling unsettled. I went to church the next morning with the question still in my mind: *How would Jesus view that conversation?* I wondered how many of those men, like myself growing up, considered themselves to be Christians purely because they went to church sometimes.

I know now that all those years I had professed to be a Christian, I was really an enemy of Christ. In the same day I might tell someone, "Sure, I'm a Christian," and moments later curse those Christians who I thought "carried faith to an extreme."

The book of James talks about a person who thinks he is religious, "and does not bridle his tongue." James says that person is deceiving his own heart, and their religion is "worthless."[39]

That was me. Before I really gave my life over to God, I was just labelling myself as a part of His family without signing the adoption papers, so to speak.

I know that God desires that all of His creation glorifies Him for all eternity, but sometimes I have to wonder about hearts like those I encountered at the party when they are entering Heaven. There is something to consider about the dignity of our faith—about the shallow labeling of Christianity for our benefit.

---

[39] James 1:26

This world and this country are filled with those who take on the label of 'Christian' when it benefits their political gain—which we see on either side of mainstream politics—and now this country is filled with those who use the label of 'Christian' to gain social justice points by declaring it a white nationalist religion to be wary of. How strange it is that the label of 'Christian' contains so much power in the world when the Christ, Himself, came to the world and lived the humblest of lives.

If we are going to engage in Civil Disobedience while taking on the label of Christianity, we should also engage in disobedience against our own flesh. If we are publicly representing God and acting in ways that make a statement against worldly mandates, we cannot also have public or private interactions that dishonor Him. Although we all sin when left to our own devices, we have to be cautious of how our actions might muddy the image of what Christianity truly looks like.

With our tongues bridled and our faith strong, we can engage in Civil Disobedience that honors God above all else.

So regardless of how many wonderful police officers exist, the problem is found among those select ones who have ugly hearts. As we have seen, there have been those who behave unjustly toward minority races; and, in this instance, that has caused a rise of fear and anger.[40] As it was pushed down, it built and then erupted.

---

[40] As a law student working for a lawyer with the NAACP, I saw countless examples of wrongdoing to minorities that explains the fear and anger caused to those minorities. Some of these situations are absolutely terrible, and God must change the heart of those who abuse anyone for the color of their skin.

The result of that was a segment of people protesting in such a way that caused chaos and violence. Their actions led to another segment of people feeling the need to lash out in response.

If one group had been willing to change their hearts, the next group would not have gone underground with their anger and hate. But they did. And once they couldn't stay under any longer, they unleashed in violence. It becomes a wagon wheel rolling down the mountain, wobbling to each side faster and faster until it crashes at the end.

With the violence that erupted on January 6, 2021, the name of God was dragged into the headlines as something to be hated. He was not glorified. He and His people were vilified.

We are meant to be ambassadors for Christ, as seen in 2 Corinthians 5:20. Anything less is an abandonment of our role on this earth. We are not ambassadors for our race. We are not ambassadors for justice. We are not ambassadors for our nation, our family, our unions, our universities, or our own souls. And similar to ambassadors of foreign nations, we know that our home isn't here, but we have to represent our Kingdom nevertheless.

We are here to represent Jesus and share His love.

CHAPTER THREE:

Disobedience is Not the Answer in All Things

HAVING LOOKED AT EXAMPLES OF WHAT CIVIL DISOBEDIENCE should look like from a Christian perspective and aspects of the heart behind it, it is also important that we recognize what it should not look like.

Yes, there are times when disobedience is done purely out of a selfish motive, but there are quite a few examples of when it should not be enacted; and if we can identify those things, we are able to better discern what is driving our own hearts.

Violence Can be an Answer

What we do need to recognize about Civil Disobedience is something that Thoreau was unafraid to discuss and that is the fact that violence can be an answer to injustice. As mentioned in the previous chapter—and before this section is misconstrued—Christians are called to methods of peace for a number of reasons.

However, being an important aspect of this topic, looking at this issue can help us in understanding the ideology behind it.

St. Augustine of Hippo may have been a man of peace and deep theology, but he was also known for his Just War Theory, in which he stated that war can, at times, be justified for purposes of justice and the greater good of the people.

While a Just War is not the same as a Holy War (such as the Islamic Jihad with which Just War is often confused), this is the sort of war in which we might categorize those fought by Israel in the Old Testament. Throughout the many instances when God led His people into battle against nations and kings who were an affront to His Name, the Just War Theory is applicable because the wars were fought for a great cause and a great justice—such as preserving the glory of the name of God.

Of course, we see many instances of Israel abusing these opportunities, but Augustine was stressing the importance of fighting against those in conflict with what the Lord commanded for His people. While Just War is neither pacifist nor nationalist, it does agree that there are times when the tragedy of war is unavoidable for the sake of an important circumstance.

As time has moved forward, there have been additional structures added to the original Just War Theory, such as the pillars that the war must be declared by a legitimate authority, the cause of the war must be just, the war should be fought with the right intention, and it must be the absolute last resort. There are also those who say that there must be a reasonable hope of justice as a means of avoiding entering wars which will ultimately be lost, wasting the lives and resources of those caught in the midst of battle.[41]

What does this look like carried out?

One of the prime examples is that of World War II. This was a war declared by multiple legitimate authorities, and it certainly appeared to be fought out of justice, particularly when we examine it from what we know of Nazi Germany's treatment of the Jews. Presumably, the war was fought with the right intention of freeing people from suffering. And with so many people having been brainwashed, it certainly appeared to be the last resort. Beyond all of that, there was a very reasonable hope of success in overcoming the enemy.

In this circumstance, a war was the best choice justice had to defeat evil. It was, absolutely, just. The idea is expressed through the Latin, *jus ad bellum/jus in bello*, which refer to the governing body that allows for war (i.e. the right to war) and the conduct shown by those who do battle with one another (i.e. justice in war).

Of course, World War II was not only the result of the Allies fighting against Nazi Germany. There were numerous battles, including the preceding Second Italo-Ethiopian War, in which Ethiopia defended themselves against colonization and brutality; the Spanish Civil War; the invasion of Japan into China; and numerous other occupations, conflicts, and disagreements.

With examples like these, we can also acknowledge that extreme pacifism isn't always the right answer. There are absolutely times

---

[41] Langan John. "The Elements of St. Augustine's Just War Theory." *The Journal of Religious Ethics*, vol 12, no 1, 1984 pp 19-38. JSTOR, www.jstor.org/stable/40014967. Accessed 8 Mar 2021

when violence can be used as the last resort. However, it is very rare for us as Christians to be called to that.[42]

When viewed through the eyes of history, we can see multiple wars fought by right and with justice. In times like these, violence can absolutely be an answer. It can be used as a method of ensuring that justice prevails and right things flourish.

Violence is not the Best Way

We can also see throughout history, however, that violence and uprising against tyranny or injustice can be done through means that are *not* honoring to Augustine's Just War Theory. Oftentimes, even in the midst of oppression and evil, violence has been used to create only more chaos and cruelty.

Take, for instance, the LA riots of 1965 and 1992.

In 1965, Watts—an area in Los Angeles, California—was rife with tension, poverty, and racial segregation. The people were justifiably frustrated by their circumstances and lack of help from the government and others in order to give them a hand up and enable the community to overcome their poverty.

So when accusations of police brutality and a citizen resisting arrest came to a head, the result was a dramatic and ugly conclusion. The riots led to the deaths of 34 people and over a thousand injured, in addition to more than 3,400 being arrested.

---

[42] General Boykin is a great example of a Christian soldier using his faith during his service, including some of the most daring military events in modern history. His book *Never Surrender: A Soldier's Journey to The Crossroads of Faith and Freedom* is a great autobiographical account.

What happened in Watts was a nasty display of injustice and oppression that built over time. Once the tension boiled over—with Officer Lee Minikus attempting to arrest Marquette Frye for drunk driving, sparking a violent incident and leading to the ensuing riots— it was impossible to ignore the overwhelming anger, hurt, and suffering of the people in a community.[43]

However, this came at great cost to that very same community and to the lives and families of those who lost loved ones, businesses, and homes. And while these riots did lead to a few policy changes for Watts in terms of education and job opportunities, it didn't take long for history to repeat itself.

In 1992, The Rodney King Riots took place, also in Los Angeles County. Once more sparked by accusations of the police using excessive force during an arrest and resistance to an arrest, the officers were acquitted of all charges despite their own Chief of Police, Daryl Gates, condemning the incident.

With this acquittal came the riots.

Sixty-four people lost their lives—and none of them were law enforcement. The very people who instigated the uprising were among its victims. With more than two-thousand injuries and over twelve-thousand arrests, these riots were an even greater display of what happens when violence is used as the answer to injustice.

While these events contributed to the efforts of President Lyndon B. Johnson's war on poverty, and money sent to LA from the Clinton administration, they never had a full effect, and they did

---

[43] History.com Editors. "Watts rebellion." *History.com*, A &E Television Networks, 28 Sept. 2017, www.history.com/topics/1960s/watts-riots

nothing to move in the hearts of the oppressors. Changing policy does not change hearts and, once more, it can only force the hate to go underground.

As we are reminded in Jeremiah 17:9,

> *The heart is deceitful above all things,*
> *and desperately sick;*
> *who can understand it?*

Deceptive hearts often lead to wrong actions and wrong motivations. Our desire to do what we want against injustice can lead to so many poor decisions when not tempered with the guidance of the Lord.

Deception is funny. When we are being deceived, we don't realize it. Deception only works if we do not know it. How can it work any other way? So, when our heart deceives us, we truly feel we are doing the right thing and have no idea that we are being led down a wrong path. It really adds to the Proverb, "Above all else, guard your heart"[44]

These instances of civil unrest show us just how ineffective violence can be when used as a tactic of reclaiming justice. What happened in LA County and the way the officers behaved was inexcusable, but the ensuing violence only served to increase division and hurt those who were already struggling under their circumstances.

---

[44] Proverbs 4:23

Interestingly, during the growth of the church for the first several hundred years, Christians did not engage in violence to spread the message of the Gospel. The Gospel message spread from suffering at the hands of those who were against Christians.

In these examples, hate breeds more hate. Very little justice is actually being served. These are not examples of Just War because, ultimately, only violence and chaos were demonstrated on both sides. More people were injured as a result, particularly among the citizens who decided to stand up and fight back.

What the Bible Has to Say about It

In Genesis 22, we read the story of Abraham taking his son, Isaac, to the mountains in the land of Moriah. There, he was meant to sacrifice his one and only son because God spoke to him and said, "Take your son, your only son Isaac, whom you love, and go to the land of Moriah, and offer him there as a burnt offering on one of the mountains of which I shall tell you."

Out of obedience to the Lord, Abraham believed that he was being called to an act of violence. He was being called to sacrifice the promised son, whom he had loved dearly and had waited for—well, aside from having an affair with his wife's maid to try and force God's hand in giving him a son.

Following the covenant of the New Testament and the work of Jesus, we can see that this was just an example to foreshadow the sacrifice of Jesus. However, for Abraham this was an order. It was an instruction that he had been given by God.

We cannot know what was going on in Abraham's mind. He may have been grieving, sad to lose his son. He may have been angry, wondering why God would give him a son and make all those promises about descendants just to take Isaac away from him. Or, he may have been perfectly fine, trusting in the nature of the one true God and believing that He would not force Abraham to carry out this heinous act.

But whatever was in Abraham's mind, we read,

> And Isaac said to his father Abraham, "My father!" And he said, "Here I am, my son." He said, "Behold, the fire and the wood, but where is the lamb for a burnt offering?" Abraham said, "God will provide for himself the lamb for a burnt offering, my son." So they went both of them together.
>
> When they came to the place of which God had told him, Abraham built the altar there and laid the wood in order and bound Isaac his son and laid him on the altar, on top of the wood. Then Abraham reached out his hand and took the knife to slaughter his son. But the angel of the Lord called to him from heaven and said, "Abraham, Abraham!" And he said, "Here I am." He said, "Do not lay your hand on the boy or do anything to him, for now I know that you fear God, seeing you have not withheld your son, your only son, from me." And Abraham lifted up his eyes and looked,

and behold, behind him was a ram, caught in a thicket by his horns. And Abraham went and took the ram and offered it up as a burnt offering instead of his son. So Abraham called the name of that place, "The Lord will provide"; as it is said to this day, "On the mount of the Lord it shall be provided." [45]

An important thing for us to note is that, no matter what God instructed Abraham from the beginning, He was faithful to avoid senseless violence. He fulfilled His promise, granting Isaac life and giving Abraham offspring.

Abraham felt that he would be brought back to life, but he knew that regardless of the consequences, he had to be obedient to God's Word. His faith was the guiding force, not his feelings.[46]

No. This was a foreshadowing of the horror of what it means for a father to sacrifice his beloved son. It also allowed for God to provide a lamb and to demonstrate the need for a sacrifice in our place.

When tempted to violate God's law, even for the right reasons, we must remain faithful in knowing that God will provide.

But God did *not* call Abraham to violence in this circumstance. If we feel that we are being drawn into such a circumstance that may require a sacrifice, death, or violence, we must remember that the Lord will provide the covering on our behalf.

---

[45] Genesis 22:7–14
[46] Hebrews 11:17-19

When Anger is Not Sparked but Planned

The Oklahoma City Bombing is an example of what happens when violence is used for the sake of one's belief in justice, but ultimately leads to death and destruction. Timothy McVeigh and his accomplices were anti-government extremists with firm beliefs that they had to fight against corruption in the American government.

One of the greatest terrorist attacks of U.S. history prior to 9-11, the bombing led to the deaths of 168 people, injuring at least 680 others. Among these victims were many children.

There was extensive damage across the city, with hundreds of buildings damaged, destroyed, or brought to the point that they had to be demolished. Ultimately Timothy McVeigh paid the price of his act through death by lethal injection. He was said to have been inspired to commit these crimes due to how the police handled the incidents at Ruby Ridge[47] and Waco[48].

In response to the excessive force employed by government officials against these men, Timothy McVeigh decided to retaliate by setting off the bomb that took the lives of innocent people and ultimately led to his own death. If he had chosen a method of nonviolence over anarchy, it is possible that people would have truly listened to what he had to say.[49]

---

[47] A standoff with the white supremacist-associated Weaver Family in Naples, Idaho, which led to the death of Vicki Weaver and 14-year-old Sammy Weaver and U.S. Marshall William Degan

[48] A government siege against the religious sect known as Branch Davidians, led by David Koresh, leading to the deaths of 76 people, including children and pregnant women.

[49] History.com Editors. "Oklahoma City Bombing" *History.com*, A&E Television Networks, 20 May. 2020, www.history.com/topics/1990s/oklahoma-city-bombing

And if we examine the Freeman Movement, we can see that there are those who believe that the law may be taken into their own hands to do as they wish. They believe that they are subject to the law based only on their own interpretation of the law and their willingness to consent to the law.

For them, rising against the government and refusing to comply with the law of the land is not out of a need for justice or a righteous revolution. It is, most often, a way of attempting to avoid responsibility.[50]

As Christians, we are called to be subject to our governing authorities. This is where the difference lies between Christian Civil Disobedience and disobedience that is not Christian (and sometimes not Civil) and simply breaking the law. Oftentimes, when people attempt to justify anarchy and violence from a Christian perspective, they will remind us of Jesus turning over tables in the temple. But did He do this out of frustration for Himself or out of a righteous fury that the Father's holy place was being blasphemed out of greed? Although God Himself, Jesus was not outraged for His own glory, but for His Father's.

This anarchic thinking allows a person to disobey whatever they want for the sake of doing whatever they want whenever they want and for whatever reason they may have. It gives us an out—a chance to disregard all proper recourse and claim that, by whatever justifying

---

[50] Fleming, Joseph Z., and Peter Demos. "Recent Developments in Emerging Crisis Law: The Militia in the Courts: Was Walter Mitty a Freeman?" *The Urban Lawyer* vol 28, no 4, 1996, pp 631-639. JSTOR, www.jstor.org/stable/27895019

means we choose, this action is important, righteous, and moral as we fight against corruption.

Anarchy, however, also ignores God's truth.

While we may believe that we can enact anarchy for the sake of our rights as inheritors of the Kingdom of God, this method goes in direct contrast to a holy, righteous anger.[51]

If we look at the Bible, the nature of systematic theology, the paths and patterns of the fall, repentance, and redemption, we can see with great clarity that God is a God of order. If we ignore that in Scripture, we can see it in the world around us, in the changing of seasons, in the ecosystems of the deserts versus those of the forests, and in the fact that our hair and fingernails grow no matter how frequently we cut them.

God is not reckless, He is not a slave to chance. He is sovereign. He does not condone chaos but constitution. So if we pursue a method that exists based on whims and frustrations, or an ideology that creates panic and disorder, we can be confident in the fact that it is not acted out in response to obedience to Him.

His methods are laid out for us in the Bible, and that is the place we can go to find them. As He leads us with clarity and truth, we will distance ourselves from an anarchist view.

Rather than enacting violence, Matthew 26:47–56 demonstrates a very different circumstance for us, saying,

---

[51] The term "righteous anger" is not mentioned in the Bible. But, it can be deduced from the cautions of David, Paul and Jesus. I would argue that righteous anger is anger which causes one to not sin. Ephesians 4:26. The motive and your fruit from the anger must not be sinful. However, recognize that when you fail, as I often have with my anger, we must repent, ask for forgiveness, and recognize that there will be consequences from it.

. . . Then they came up and laid hands on Jesus and seized him. And behold, one of those who were with Jesus stretched out his hand and drew his sword and struck the servant of the high priest and cut off his ear. Then Jesus said to him, "Put your sword back into its place. For all who take the sword will perish by the sword. Do you think that I cannot appeal to my Father, and he will at once send me more than twelve legions of angels? But how then should the Scriptures be fulfilled, that it must be so?"[52]

We are reminded once more that Jesus does not need us to defend Him. He is more than capable of defending His own Name and standing in His own right. We are called to be obedient before Him and honor Him for the sake of drawing others to Him.

The one who was with Jesus was angry and sought to defend Him from the enemies who were coming against Him. Rather than standing by and allowing anyone to hurt his Savior, this disciple tried to fight back.

But Jesus called on His disciples to stop the violence and allow Him to be taken. If He wanted legions of angels to come to His aid, they would have come in an instant.

We, too, are called to peace rather than the sword. If we fight back, we bloody the name of Jesus. If we stand up in our own

---

[52] Matthew 26:50–54

defense, we are pursuing our own justice, and we become no better than the anarchists, the rioters, and those who incite uprisings and violence.

A Place to Call Home

It is not our duty to defend our lives in this world. This is not our home, nor is it the home of Jesus. He told us this Himself in John 18:33-38.

> So Pilate entered his headquarters again and called Jesus and said to him, "Are you the King of the Jews?" Jesus answered, "Do you say this of your own accord, or did others say it to you about me?" Pilate answered, "Am I a Jew? Your own nation and the chief priests have delivered you over to me. What have you done?" Jesus answered, "My kingdom is not of this world. If my kingdom were of this world, my servants would have been fighting, that I might not be delivered over to the Jews. But my kingdom is not from the world." Then Pilate said to him, "So you are a king?" Jesus answered, "You say that I am a king. For this purpose I was born and for this purpose I have come into the world—to bear witness to the truth. Everyone who is of the truth listens to my voice." Pilate said to him, "What is truth?"

Jesus did not allow His servants to fight on His behalf. Why? Because this world is not His kingdom. This world is the place in which He dwelled for a time, but it was never meant to be His home.

Neither is it ours.

Beyond this, we look at how Jesus responded to Pilate's authority in these verses. He was, essentially, telling Pilate that he was not concerned by Pilate's title or position. Jesus was displaying His own authority and that He could be free of the punishment if He wished.

For us, this is another reminder that we do not have to fight back. Our job is to live in a way that changes the hearts of others. We want to change the hearts of others to show Christ....not to highlight our cause.

In order to proclaim the Name of Jesus, we may be called upon to engage in Civil Disobedience, but we will never be called upon to fight to defend Him against the attacks of the world. The very same world that is ruled by sin was created by Him. All Jesus needs to do is seize control of the injustice and sin; He can handle it quite well on His own, without our help.

One day, He will come and reign over all. But, until then, we must bear in mind what this world is and what it is not.

This world is not our home. If we are warriors of a Kingdom, we fight for our Kingdom. We do not fight on behalf of the enemy. We do not defend a world ruled by sin but instead proclaim that our King is the one true King.

So for us to live as we were called to live, our hope is in Christ and in living lives that are obedient to Him. No matter how just our war may appear, we have been instructed to live peacefully and to do so for the sake of honoring the name of God.

This world is remarkable in how God created it.

There are close to ten thousand different species of birds alone across the world that have been discovered. A large, towering tree can grow from a tiny acorn. There are hot, sandy oceans and cold, snowy mountains. There are melodies that are so beautiful they can make our hair stand on end. Bitter beans can be harvested to create things like coffee and chocolate. And there are millions of other incredible aspects of the world we interact with on a daily basis.

But this world is not our home, and for us to enact violence upon it is to do nothing but diminish God's determination that it is worth laying down one's life to save.

When is it Appropriate for Us to Respond?

It is easy to dismiss the frustrations and thoughts of those who do violence. 2020 is replete with examples.[53] We cannot diminish the concerns of the citizens of LA who sparked the 1965 riots, nor can we ignore that someone like Timothy McVeigh may have been correct that the government did not handle the Ruby Ridge and Waco incidents in the best manner. Right or wrong, this is irrelevant to our duty as a Christian.

But what does it mean for us in terms of how to respond?

---

[53] I include the act of January 6, 2021, in the year 2020 as it seemed to be the same actions just running a week late.

There will be times when we do have to use discernment to know when to obey and when to refuse to comply. While there are many examples to follow, it is important to note that our decision as to whether or not we need to comply with the government very much depends on what God has to say on an issue.

Where does the Bible stand if the government rules that you must address a trans person by their preferred pronoun as opposed to the gender that God created in their DNA? What if your government asks you to kill an ethnic group? What if they forced you to have an abortion due to population control or because your baby might have Down Syndrome? What if they promoted the slave trade? And should we stop attending church as a congregation on Sunday mornings because the governor mandates it, despite the fact that we are called in Scripture to not neglect our meeting together?

These questions are not simply dilemmas to discuss in an ethics class—like *is it wrong to steal bread to feed your family?* Rather, these are instances that Christians have to be prepared to face. We have already been warned that things are going to grow more difficult in the days to come. While it is crucial that we do not respond by rallying our church members and storming the capitol or the governor's office, we do have to be prepared with discernment and a right understanding of how to respond and under what circumstances.

CHAPTER FOUR:

Civil Disobedience as a Christian When Asked to Commit Evil

THROUGHOUT HISTORY, WE HAVE SEEN EXAMPLES OF CHRISTIANS being asked to commit evil. But what exactly does this mean? How can we determine what is and isn't evil?

For instance, paying taxes is different from committing murder. In the U.S., it is true that some of our tax dollars go to funding abortive procedures, but some tax dollars also go to caring for the 'least of these' and the Bible instructs us to 'give to Caesar,'[54] so paying taxes when the government is in a constant, back-and-forth battle over whether or not it will go toward organizations who perform abortions isn't necessarily the same as us engaging to commit murder.

---

[54] Mark 12:17

When Jesus said that taxes should be paid to Caesar, recognize that Caesar Tiberius was a ruthless man who not only viewed himself as a god but also was known to molest young children, both boys and girls, and have them thrown off the island of Capri when they got too old.[55]

In our western, industrialized cultural context, it may seem far-fetched to think about the government forcing us to commit evil, but this is the reality in many parts of the world. Things like forced abortions and forced euthanasia seem foreign when we live in a society that parades these things as being a choice. Unfortunately, these creeping cultural changes can sneak up on us.[56]

Isaiah 5:20 says, "Woe to those who call evil good and good evil, who put darkness for light and light for darkness, who put bitter for sweet and sweet for bitter!"

This verse warns us against calling evil good and good evil. So if we say that committing abortion is good for the sake of the future of the planet—that killing our second child means we have more resources for our first—we are justifying an evil act and declaring it an act of self-sacrifice for the good of all mankind. And, unfortunately, this is something that is being touted with great frequency.

Without getting into the contrast of God's command to be fruitful and multiply versus the modern ideology of population control for the greater good of mankind, when we look at the

---

[55] Life of Tiberius by Suetonis sections 43 and 44
[56] 1 Corinthians 5:6 "A little leaven leavens the whole lump." We don't recognize that sin slowly spreads until it is too late.

justification of evil and how it is manipulated for good, we have to be prepared with eyes wide open for how it is being used around us. But what is really scary is how it is being *normalized* and how easily that can sneak into church culture as well.

Moses and the Midwives

Most people know the Moses story, but few know who Shiphrah and Puah are. These two women through civil disobedience helped save the Jewish people from extinction by a cruel leader.

In Exodus 1:15-22, we read,

> "Then the king of Egypt said to the Hebrew midwives, one of whom was named Shiphrah and the other Puah, "When you serve as midwife to the Hebrew women and see them on the birthstool, if it is a son, you shall kill him, but if it is a daughter, she shall live." But the midwives feared God and did not do as the king of Egypt commanded them, but let the male children live. So the king of Egypt called the midwives and said to them, "Why have you done this, and let the male children live?" The midwives said to Pharaoh, "Because the Hebrew women are not like the Egyptian women, for they are vigorous and give birth before the midwife comes to them." So God dealt well with the midwives. And the people multiplied and grew very strong. And because the midwives feared God, he gave them

families. Then Pharaoh commanded all his people, "Every son that is born to the Hebrews you shall cast into the Nile, but you shall let every daughter live.'"

Shiphrah and Puah were the midwives of Moses' time. It doesn't expressly say that they were the ones who delivered this deliverer, but their boldness led to the survival of many Hebrew baby boys who would have been contemporaries of Moses.

Although they saved many Jewish boys, they did not altogether stop the murder of many more. Archeological evidence points to a disproportionately large number of women who were buried over men.[57]

We know that lying is a sin and, chances are, Shiphrah and Puah didn't just so happen to miss *every* birth of a baby boy among the Hebrews. But would their lie have been a greater evil than committing the murder of God's chosen people? Certainly not!

And yet, they stood their ground. They refused to follow the evil they were asked to commit, choosing instead not to kill these children; and they gave another reason. Through this act of civil disobedience, God rewarded them. Because of their refusal to murder the children of Israel, He blessed them. Their refusal to do evil—their stand against infanticide—was grounds for giving them life in abundance with families of their own.[58]

---

[57] Patterns of Evidence: The Exodus. Timothy P. Mahoney. Kevin Sorbo, Timothy P. Mahoney, Michael Medved: Thinking Man Films, 2015 Minneapolis Minnesota

[58] Note that this is not 'works-based' theology. God is not obligated to reward our obedience with anything other than the eternity with Him, which is the greatest gift we can imagine. But it is possible that our eternity with Him come after the edge of a sword or a season of suffering.

This is one of the earliest accounts we have of God-fearing people being in a position where the leader of the land is forcing them to commit evil, but they resisted. We must do the same.

For those who live in modern Western culture, this may seem farfetched, but change is rarely a light switch that turns on and off. It is rather a dimmer knob that slowly increases of decreases until you no longer recognize it. In 2019, Governors of New York, Rhode Island, and Virginia advocated abortions while a baby is in the birth canal if the baby will be deformed or deemed "unable to survive"[59]

Whatever our field of employment may call us to do, we must be prepared to give an account for the vigorous nature of God's people. This is a boldness we have to cling to with wisdom and obedience, knowing that the Lord is always going to help us as we stand firm.

Obadiah

Not to be confused with the book of Obadiah the Prophet, this story in 1 Kings 18 gives us an insight into the life of the prophet Elijah, while showing us another man's remarkable obedience to God. It says,

> "And Ahab called Obadiah, who was over the household. (Now Obadiah feared the Lord greatly, and when Jezebel cut off the prophets of the Lord, Obadiah took a hundred prophets and hid them by fifties in a

---

[59] "Horror: Virginia Governor Says It's Okay to Kill a Baby after It is Born" The Yeshiva World January 30, 2019 and Ramesh Ponnuru, "The infanticide Craze" National Review January 30, 2019

cave and fed them with bread and water.) And Ahab said to Obadiah, "Go through the land to all the springs of water and to all the valleys. Perhaps we may find grass and save the horses and mules alive, and not lose some of the animals." So they divided the land between them to pass through it. Ahab went in one direction by himself, and Obadiah went in another direction by himself."[60]

Already, we are told that Obadiah has disobeyed Jezebel once before in an effort to care for the Lord's prophets. He risked his own life for the sake of obedience to God and his fear of the Lord.

Although we know very little about this man and this story is brief, he provided for God's chosen people when they were being sought out and systematically killed by a woman who was known for her evil deeds.

But in this story, Obadiah is given another chance to choose obedience to the Lord. Faced with an enemy of the nation's rulers, he had a choice to make.

"And as Obadiah was on the way, behold, Elijah met him. And Obadiah recognized him and fell on his face and said, "Is it you, my lord Elijah?" And he answered him, "It is I. Go, tell your lord, 'Behold, Elijah is here.'" And he said, "How have I sinned, that you

---

[60] 1 Kings 18:3–6

would give your servant into the hand of Ahab, to kill me? As the Lord your God lives, there is no nation or kingdom where my lord has not sent to seek you. And when they would say, 'He is not here,' he would take an oath of the kingdom or nation, that they had not found you. And now you say, 'Go, tell your lord, "Behold, Elijah is here."' And as soon as I have gone from you, the Spirit of the Lord will carry you I know not where. And so, when I come and tell Ahab and he cannot find you, he will kill me, although I your servant have feared the Lord from my youth. Has it not been told my lord what I did when Jezebel killed the prophets of the Lord, how I hid a hundred men of the Lord's prophets by fifties in a cave and fed them with bread and water? And now you say, 'Go, tell your lord, "Behold, Elijah is here"'; and he will kill me." And Elijah said, "As the Lord of hosts lives, before whom I stand, I will surely show myself to him today." So Obadiah went to meet Ahab, and told him. And Ahab went to meet Elijah."[61]

Once more trusting in God to be faithful—and trusting Elijah to do the same, Obadiah chose obedience. He refused to hand Elijah over in such a way that Elijah would be killed but instead allowed Elijah to present himself on his own terms.

---

[61] 1 Kings 18:7–16

This act of civil disobedience illustrates a situation where our leaders ask us as individuals to hand over specific people—to call them out for their piety, their religious beliefs, their political affiliations, or other things that are not inherently evil. If we comply, we commit treason against the people of God.

It is absolutely evil to engage in the systematic destruction of a people, and if God calls us in obedience to be the ones who hide His people in caves and feed them, we have no choice but to honor Him by doing so.

Unfortunately, today we see the beginning pains of this as well; and sometimes it appears within the church.

What we are seeing often in the current church climate is the use of Jesus' name to defend our respective political ideologies. This is never something we should stand for.

Whether the conservative politicians call upon conservative Christians to 'out' their liberal brothers (because ALL liberal Christians "want to kill babies") or whether the liberal politicians call upon liberal Christians to 'out' their conservative brothers (because ALL conservative Christians "hate immigrants"), we need to boldly stand against it.

We cannot fall into a trap like this. Again, it may seem farfetched, but just as Jezebel wanted the prophets to be exposed, even by God-fearing Jews, we are seeing trends even through social media in which God-fearing Christians are being exposed based on which candidate they prefer or a political stance they take.

If we give in to this kind of evil wherein we are dividing the Church for the sake of loyalty to our government, we are not respecting the allegiances we have been called to through the Bible. It is for no one's greater good that we engage in evil, and we must continue to distinguish the two from a Biblical perspective.

The Holocaust

There are, perhaps, few better-known horrifying events in modern history than the Holocaust. This was a time of great evil—a time when a government rose up and systematically, mercilessly destroyed two-thirds of Europe's Jewish population, in addition to some five-million other lives who were considered "undesirables." And while it was hardly the only genocide in history, it was one which should give Christians pause for thought.

It is ghastly to think that among the Nazi leaders and collaborators, there were many Christian leaders who failed to love their fellow humans and gave themselves up to nationalism over morality, or even defended the radical destruction of Jews for their culpability in the crucifixion of Jesus.[62] They accepted evil rather than standing against it.[63]

Doris Bergen, an expert in Holocaust history, noted that during this season in Germany, approximately 95% of German citizens had

---

[62] This ideology is extremely dangerous for many reasons, but among them, we must remember that a) the Jews of today were not actively shouting, "Crucify him!" some 2000 years ago, and b) it was in God's sovereignty that He came in human form to give up His life for our justification. Without the death on the cross, there would be no salvation and we would not be counted as righteous or be among God's chosen people—unless we are Jewish.

[63] Cline, Austin. "Hitler, Nationalism, and Positive Christianity." Learn Religions, 16 February 2021, learnreligions.com/adolf-hitler-and-christian-ationalism-248189.

been baptized as Christians.[64] They were not advocates of postmodern mentalities that diminish the role of church and Christianity, nor did they profess that it was their own version of truth that led them into the willingness to subject Holocaust victims to their suffering. There were, reportedly, sermons preached against Jews, and the government made its way into the church with ease.

However, there were Christians who stood firmly against evil, even when it wasn't popular. Even when the Church sided with the government (and when Hitler used the German Church for his own benefit), there were those who understood the dangers of this mentality and fought against it.

Dietrich Bonhoeffer declared this as evil and was even a courier for an organization that was plotting the assassination of Hitler. Although it is debated as to how much of the plot he was involved in, Bonhoeffer nevertheless was bold enough to stand firm when it was unpopular to do so.[65]

He put himself in harm's way to fight against this evil that he was being asked to commit. Repeatedly, Bonhoeffer had been offered and asked to go against his conscience. His stand against Naziism was something he'd been given many opportunities to practice before. He had already made decisions and taken stands that made him

---

[64] To learn more about the strength of the German Christian Movement and the impact it had on helping the Nazi's genocide against the Jewish people, I recommend the through account of the German Christians in Bergen's book, The Twisted Cross: The German Christian Movement in the Third Reich, University of North Carolina Press 1996.
https://ffrf.org/legal/item/12749-the-christian-soil-of-the-holocaust-part-ii
https://nationalpost.com/holy-post/military-chaplains-caught-between-word-of-god-and-horror-of-man
[65] Ibid p1

unpopular in the German and the American Churches, firmly denouncing progressivist influence on Christianity.[66]

But his stand against Hitler's indoctrination cost him his life. After being arrested by the Gestapo, he was executed at the Flossenbürg concentration camp.

This is a stark contrast to the prosperous family lives of Shripha and Puah, but we can take comfort in knowing that Bonhoeffer, Shripha, and Puah—regardless of their lives here on earth—have all found themselves in the same place after their deaths. And if we stand firm in obedience and in fearing God, we will find ourselves there one day as well.

The Holocaust was a challenge to many Christians who were called upon to be a part of something evil that was packaged to appear as a benefit for a specific society. If the day is not already here, it will certainly come soon when we, as well, will have to choose whether or not to follow the laws of the land by exposing those who are considered 'undesirable' or refuse to give in to evil—even if it costs us our lives.

The Only Prophet Left

If we return to 1 Kings and look at the events that followed from Obadiah and Elijah, there is a striking statement that Elijah gives us.

"I, even I only, am left a prophet of the Lord, but Baal's prophets are 450 men."[67]

---

[66] Ibid p 12
[67] 1 Kings 18:22

And later, "He said, 'I have been very jealous for the Lord, the God of hosts. For the people of Israel have forsaken your covenant, thrown down your altars, and killed your prophets with the sword, and I, even I only, am left, and they seek my life, to take it away.'"[68]

Elijah lived a life that was lonely. He was the only prophet left who was willing to speak truth in Israel. The other prophets either refused to speak or they had turned away. Instead, Elijah was faced with the prophets of Baal and Asherah.

Eventually, God granted him the companionship of Elisha, but prior to that, Elijah was obedient even unto severe isolation. Jezebel, the queen, was eagerly trying to murder him, and Elijah begged God to let him die.

When we choose to stand against evil, we have to be ready for the consequences. But rather than giving in and worshiping idols and other gods, we can look to Elijah who refused to commit such a sin against God—even when his life was threatened by the governing authorities.

He was unwilling to lay down and do evil. Instead, Elijah chose to worship God and to expose evil for what it really was. He spoke out against idolatry and the sin that Israel had so easily accepted.

The Weeping Prophet

The prophet Jeremiah in the Bible is described as 'the weeping prophet' for all of his hardship and endurance. But Jeremiah had reason to weep.

---

[68] 1 Kings 19:10

He wept not only because of the immense persecution he faced at the hands of the church leaders and other prophets, but he also wept for his grief in their disobedience to God.

Jeremiah faced plots against him[69], as well as beatings, gossip, and mocking[70]. He struggled through all manner of difficulties resulting from his dedication to God's call upon his life. He even spoke of times when he tried to refrain from prophesying and how it burned in his heart.

But when we are faced with trials and persecution for speaking the truth, even when our government leaders and certainly when our church leaders say it is wrong of us, we are still urged to trust God and to engage in Civil Disobedience as it pertains to refusing to give in to idolatry.

And when we weep for the suffering we are facing, we must also weep for the blaspheming of God's name. The last thing we want to see is for unbelievers to have a false perspective of who God is because cultural Christians are displaying a weak version of Him.

If cultural Christians show a version of God who is happy to sit by and allow everyone their own truth, that is the version of God that unbelievers will see. It is a version that should grieve us, and in obedience we have to stand up and declare that truth is not our choice. Truth is what God says it is, even if what He has declared to be true is not the popular thing that people want to hear.

---

[69] Jeremiah 11
[70] Jeremiah 20

81

Call it Something Else and They'll Think It's Okay

"What has been is what will be,

and what has been done is what will be done,

and there is nothing new under the sun."

This poem from Ecclesiastes 1:9 has some frightening connotations, but it is very true. There is nothing new under the sun; but evil things often get a new name and are then accepted.

For instance, slavery was an evil, barbaric practice that took place for millennia, leading up to the end of slavery during the Abolitionist movement in England and the Civil War in America. Slavery as it was then is now over.

Except that it's not.

Although the phrase "human trafficking" still has a negative connotation, it is far more palatable than the term "slavery." And the reality is, there are and always will be new versions of it that are defended. The Department of Homeland Security used to define Human Trafficking as, "Human trafficking is modern-day slavery and involves the use of force, fraud, or coercion to obtain some type of labor or commercial sex act." But recently they modified the definition to exclude "modern-day slavery." This should deeply disturb us.

Further, political alliances have resulted in a decrease in Human Trafficking Rankings as the US allegedly has turned its head away from allegations regarding slavery when trade routes and other treaties have taken place.[71]

Even in the debate over sweat shops and unfair labor practices in the garment industry, there are those who defend it with the reminder that at least these people have jobs and are getting *something*.

They ignore the fact that the fast fashion industry is rife with unsafe work conditions, leading to events like the Rana Plaza Incident[72] and others. The "employees" in places like this are often stuck, unable to leave this work even though they are not making enough to get by and are often forced into debt by their employers—a debt they will never be able to work themselves out of so that they are working and never seeing the money as it all goes to pay a debt. Meanwhile, they are accruing more debt through things like meals provided in the workplace or, perhaps, a place to live.

And what happens when 'undesirables' are the ones driven into work camps or some sort of labor which is justified as having the purpose of benefiting them or the culture somehow? Will we call it a "reeducation camp" in which those whose views are considered "problematic" are taught to think in a way that agrees with how the government has taught society to think?

But slavery is not the only thing that can easily be rebranded. All types of unjust behaviors are easy to sell as something good.

---

[71] Jennifer Teng "Is the Government playing politics with Human Trafficking Rankings?" Washington Examiner July 31, 2015. This article addresses the new standings after trade agreements were made with Malaysia, Cuba, and Thailand. Although the US has denied this, the timing of it has made this suspect.

[72] The Rana Plaza Incident on April 24, 2013 was the collapse of a Bangladeshi garment factory that led to the deaths of 1,134 people who had pleaded with their bosses for safer work conditions. The employees were paid well below a living wage, had their concerns ignored, and were threatened with being fired. Many also expressed issues with sexual harassment in the workplace.

If you watch a documentary about ancient societies who practiced child sacrifice, you will get a grisly image of a barbaric act. However, sacrificing the life of a child for any gain is still child sacrifice. If a woman wants to further her career, and she believes that she is incapable of doing that if motherhood gets in the way, what does she do when she becomes pregnant unexpectedly?

We certainly cannot say that she sacrifices her child for the sake of her own convenience, because that is not a palatable thing to say. But to offer her "the empowering choice of abortion" (or "reproductive justice") sounds like something that benefits her and society as a whole.

This type of rebranding is a genius manipulation. It convinces us that evil is good and that even we, as Christians, can support it. When the government calls upon church leaders to pray a blessing over an abortion clinic[73], and when those church leaders agree, they are serving a purpose whereby their commitment to their political doctrines is greater than their belief in what the Bible states quite clearly—that we are knit in our mother's womb. And this means that the act of abortion is the very definition of child sacrifice.

What other evil has been rebranded? Furthermore, how might that new image lead to us being forced to do something that violates God's law?

We can see this choice faced by Christians who teach science in the public school system. They must teach the Big Bang Theory as

---

[73] There have been MANY instances of this in recent times. What these leaders all have in common is a commitment to progressivism in the church and, often, a commitment to inclusive faith (or the idea that all roads lead to God).

fact even if they believe in the literal Genesis account of creation. A friend of mine, Shawn, has a daughter who, while attending Middle School at a local school, was surprised to see his daughter was marked off for answering a test question that God created the Earth. The daughter, knowing the answer, was willing to change it to "Big Bang," which is what the teacher wanted, so she could get a good grade.

After explaining to her that she would not get in trouble for staying true to the Truth, she kept the answer the same, and the teacher marked it off.

Shawn, recognizing that something was not right, decided to sit in on a classroom setting so he could see the lessons being taught. He heard the teacher tell the children that it was wrong for the parents to pass down their beliefs (presumably about God) to these children and made the children raise their hands if they would agree with that statement.

After confronting the principal about it, he recognized there was no change, so he would visit the school often, talking to the teachers and sharing the Gospel with the kids in the cafeteria. Although he is unaware of any conversions among the teachers, they started calling on him to show boys how to tie ties and be a great support to others.

Unfortunately, this is not a limited occurrence of the world inoculating culture with ideas that violate God's law.

We can see it overseas in Iceland which boasts of having eradicated Down's Syndrome when in reality they have simply implemented a culture in which extra chromosomes are not tolerated and must be destroyed. This idea ultimately led to forced sterilization of tens of thousands of women.[74] Without God, those in power can determine what is truth and ultimately use their power to hide evil through their version of truth.[75]

There are many ways in which Satan attacks through the government, but what we have to realize is that this is not the end of it.

At the moment, Christians are being shown that we are not special. We do not receive special treatment for our beliefs and, as time goes on, we are being shown more and more how intolerable our beliefs are. While many politicians still make every effort to boast their Christianity for the sake of votes, there are plenty who have done so while touting deeply anti-Christian doctrine.

Beyond that, there are many more politicians who are now stealing away from Christianity altogether and following more progressive religions or their own self-identity, which allows them to claim whatever beliefs they hold dear as convenient to their life.

The book of Revelation has been interpreted in so many different ways by so many different men and women from so many different theological backgrounds. One thing that we can all agree on is that the book of Revelation addresses that believers in Christ *will* face a

---

[74] Thomas Williams, "Aborting Babies with Down Syndrome Equates to Eugenics" Brieibart November 22 2020; Julian Quinones and Arijeta Lajka "'What kind of society do you want to live in?' Inside the country where Down Syndrome is disappearing." CBSNews August 14, 2017
[75] For example, Margaret Sanger, in advocating for abortion, stated in her book *Pivot of Civilization*, "Evidences of biological and racial degeneracy are apparent to this observer. 'Compared with the African negro,' she writes, 'the British sub-man is in several respects markedly inferior. He tends to be dull; he is usually quite helpless and unhandy; he has, as a rule, no skill or knowledge of handicraft, or indeed knowledge of any kind.... Over-population is a phenomenon connected with the survival of the unfit, and it is mechanism which has created conditions favorable to the survival of the unfit and the elimination of the fit.'"

time when we are forced to worship an anti-Christ, whether that is a man or a doctrine or some other entity.

No matter where we are in the last days, whether we are ten days from the end or a thousand years from the end, we are drawing ever closer to the time when we are forced to choose who and what we will worship. We each must choose whether our hearts remain obedient to God or whether we surrender to the political schemes of Satan and participate in evil.

The Civil Disobedience of Shripha and Puah saved the lives of Jewish children, and God counted it to them as righteousness. The Civil Disobedience of Obadiah led to the safety of a hundred prophets. The Civil Disobedience of Dietrich Bonhoeffer led to the life-saving rescue of Jews and the softening of hearts, and his martyrdom is still impacting Christians today. The Civil Disobedience of Elijah led to marvelous works in which God's glory was on display for all to see. The Civil Disobedience of Jeremiah ultimately, and after his death, contributed to the people of Israel turning back to God.

In these examples we see some who were blessed in this life and others who merely suffered. But, again, one thing they all have in common is that they are, even now, rejoicing before the throne of God above.

Because the deceptions of Satan are clever and scheming, and because he recycles the same evils packaged in new ways, we must always be on our guard. Rather than studying what is false, we have to study what is true. In order to know whether or not something is evil, we have to understand God's law.

The only way to truly obey God's law is to be able to recognize when something violates it. When we see that something is doing just that, we can stand against it and declare the truth even if that isn't popular, even if the government says we are not allowed, and even when the church has decided that it is somehow wrong.

The practical implementations of this are studying God's Word, being discerning of the Christian leaders we follow, and praying for wisdom as we move forward in the world and seek to engage with the lost to show them the true nature of God.

If He calls us to civil disobedience in order to denounce evil, that is exactly what we must do. Whether it leads us to a life of prosperity or to the early death of a martyr, we will ultimately have the joy of standing before His throne at the end of our days.

Chapter Five

When a Governing Law Violates God's Law

In the previous chapter, we looked at what it means when the government commands us to do evil, but what about when the government prevents us from doing good? This, too, is a dilemma we as believers must face.

Without God, those that have power become the arbiters of "truth." Government will use various techniques to silence the Word of God. In parts of China, landlords are pressured to stop renting to Christians; and in India, the leading Hindu Nationalist Bharatiya Janata Party have tried to impose anti-conversion laws. They have encouraged the murder of Christians, in some cases even by their own parents.[76]

In the United States, perceived "hate speech" starts the process to attack Christians. In 1972, George Carlin made history with his

---

[76] Gavin, Harvey. "Mapped: The 50 countries where you can't be a Christian in 2017" *Express* 11-8-2017

"Seven Words You Can Never Say on Television" by causing a case that went all the way to the Supreme Court[77] and was ruled as not violating any laws. In this case, seven "dirty" words were rattled off in a comedic monologue—seven words that made people very uncomfortable. In our modern climate, many of these words can be heard on regular broadcasts, without causing a single blush. Things change quickly and quietly, and we need to be prepared.

Recently, we have seen how the gathering together of believers has been attacked since 2020 in the name of prevention against a virus. Although we see plagues in the Old Testament and know of more to come in Revelation, God's Word never gives us instructions for a pandemic. Yes, there are responsibilities we have to maybe miss a Sunday or two if we are very ill and do not wish to endanger others in our congregation, but that is not the same as bowing to a government ruling that forces the closure of our churches for an extended period of time.

Declaring certain Christian beliefs from the pulpit is now considered "hate speech"[78] in many countries, and this is rapidly spreading to new places with consequences to those pastors who remain true to orthodox Scripture. What happens when men of God are restricted from preaching the Word of God? There are two choices they must make.

The first, of course, is to remain obedient to the Lord and risk whatever fines or sentences may be passed on to them. The second is

---

[77] FCC v. Pacifica Foundation 438 US 726 (1978)
[78] Dixon, T. (2002, August 05). 'Hate speech' law could chill sermons. Retrieved April 10, 2021, from https://www.christianitytoday.com/ct/2002/august5/15.22.html

to bend the knee and preach a watered-down, progressive brand of the gospel.

But in the words of the great Scottish minister Thomas Guthrie,

> "Viewed in the light of eternity, the church stands on a loftier elevation than the palace, and the pulpit offers man a grander position than the throne of empires. To ministers of the Gospel belongs a high pre-eminence. They can say, We are fellow labourers with God. With such an associate, in such lofty company, devoting his life to so great a cause, no wonder that Paul calmly confronted a sceptical, sneering, scoffing world, and bravely said, I am not ashamed of the Gospel of Christ. I am anxious that you should understand that the honours of which I have spoken are not reserved for pulpits."[79]

This is our honor, and it is not limited to pastors but to all who follow Christ. This is the honor of all who follow Christ and have devoted our lives to Him. If we should choose to pass through life with a weak gospel narrative, we believe in a weak god. This is not the same God who created us and, with equal creativity, grace, and mercy, saved us.

---

[79] "The Gospel in Ezekiel" Thomas Guthrie, 1857. Spellings accurate to the time and place in which it was written.

Daniel and the Lions' Den

More than a Sunday school coloring page, the story of Daniel is a lesson for us all. While the miracle of God preventing the hungry lions from eating Daniel is remarkable, it is the precedent that we need to focus on in times of persecution and governing laws that violate the law of God.

What actually put Daniel in the den? We find the answer in Daniel 6, where we learn of Daniel's high position in the kingdom and how his contemporaries felt about it. In verses 4-9, we read,

> "Then the high officials and the satraps sought to find a ground for complaint against Daniel with regard to the kingdom, but they could find no ground for complaint or any fault, because he was faithful, and no error or fault was found in him. Then these men said, 'We shall not find any ground for complaint against this Daniel unless we find it in connection with the law of his God.'
>
> "Then these high officials and satraps came by agreement to the king and said to him, 'O King Darius, live forever! All the high officials of the kingdom, the prefects and the satraps, the counselors and the governors are agreed that the king should establish an ordinance and enforce an injunction, that whoever makes petition to any god or man for thirty days, except to you, O king, shall be cast into the den of lions. Now,

O king, establish the injunction and sign the document, so that it cannot be changed, according to the law of the Medes and the Persians, which cannot be revoked.' Therefore King Darius signed the document and injunction."

This was the complaint that led to Daniel's disobedience. As the chapter continues, we learn that he continued to worship the Lord with his windows open, bowing three times each day to give praise to God. These men were aware of this when they urged Darius to sign the injunction, and it was for this reason that Daniel was ultimately thrown before the lions.

We don't know what was going through Daniel's mind as he left his windows open to pray each day. We are told that he knew about the injunction that was signed—it's not as if he was taken by surprise or that he had been tricked. Instead, it is clear that this was a conscious decision Daniel made. And when they arrested him, he did not pretend to be ignorant of the new law and promise not to do it again.

What would you do? If you were told you could not pray or talk about Jesus....

Would you stop?

Would you hide?

Would you boldly refuse?

Oddly, it was Darius who was grieved and even wished Daniel deliverance by the hand of God.

How much glory it brought God to honor such a petition from a heathen! After Darius dealt rather brutally with those who tricked him into signing the injunction, he turned around and praised God, declaring that his own people should be under God and singing praises to Him.

But what if things had not gone that way? What if God would have been most glorified by Daniel's death? What if his blood as a martyr would have led others to see his great faith and desire such a kinship with God that they would give up their own lives?

Based on everything we know of Daniel, he still would have thrown open his windows and prayed three times each day. The teeth of a lion did not cause him the same fear and trembling as the justice of God.

We are obviously called to this, but we are also called to raise our families to follow this. So when our children are no longer allowed to pray in school, do we tell them to go hide in the bathroom before their lunch break and pray in there to thank God for their food? Or do we teach them to boldly bow their heads regardless of who may be sitting next to them at the lunch table?

If classroom prayer has been stripped away, does that mean that personal prayer must be as well? Absolutely not. We have to encourage the little ones in our lives to live out their faith regardless of the consequences, just as we do. This is the example that we are called to set for our children and to encourage them to live in obedience according to the law of God.

But If Not...

Daniel was not alone in being taken from his people to serve other kings. Shadrach, Meshach, and Abednego are also known for divine protection. They survived being thrown in a fiery furnace after refusing to bow in worship to a golden idol created by King Nebuchadnezzar.[80]

There is something very telling about the character of these men.

Nebuchadnezzar said to them, "But if you do not worship, you shall immediately be cast into a burning fiery furnace. And who is the god who will deliver you out of my hands?"

These three men were not the only believers. There were others with them. But, these three remained standing when the rest bowed. Imagine those believers that cowered down, who thought these three were stupid or radicals. You can almost hear the whispers—"Get down!" Imagine the fear they felt as the guards started walking toward them at the behest of an angry king.

> Shadrach, Meshach, and Abednego answered and said to the king, "O Nebuchadnezzar, we have no need to answer you in this matter. If this be so, our God whom we serve is able to deliver us from the burning fiery furnace, and he will deliver us out of your hand, O king. But if not, be it known to you, O king, that we will

---

[80] Daniel 3

not serve your gods or worship the golden image that you have set up."[81]

"But if not…"

These must always be the words we live by as we obey the Lord. We are to have faith that He will deliver us. We are to trust in His power and authority to the extent that we *know* with absolute certainty that He is capable of doing so. And yet, we must also respect that same authority to know that His sovereign will may end with us *not* being rescued.

What then? Do we cower in fear and cave to the whims of a worldly authority? Or do we say, "But if not . . . we will not serve your gods . . ."

These "gods" may look different today than they did in the times of Shadrach, Meshach, and Abednego; but they are still ever-present. The gods of "equality" and "social justice" have gone so far as urging parents to allow their children to choose their own gender at the age of five. And, shockingly so, there are those parents who have had their rights questioned as "child cruelty" if they did not bow.[82]

---

[81] Daniel 3:15b-18

[82] - Nieves, E. (2002, June 27). Judges ban pledge of allegiance from schools, citing 'under god'. Retrieved April 10, 2021, from https://www.nytimes.com/2002/06/27/us/judges-ban-pledge-of-allegiance-from-schools-citing-under-god.html

- Crossland, K. WORLD Digital. (n.d.). Parents lose custody of transgender teen. Retrieved April 10, 2021, from https://www.baptistpress.com/resource-library/news/parents-lose-custody-of-transgender-teen/

- Honderich, H. (2019, October 25). Texas parents battle in court for custody of Transgender child. Retrieved April 10, 2021, from https://www.bbc.com/news/world-us-canada-50172907

Rather than seeing the underlying mental health causes behind an increased risk of depression and suicide for those with gender dysphoria, families are cast as unsupportive and bullying if they do not fully support a transition. They are deemed to be the root cause of the drastically high numbers of depressive tendencies in transgender children.

How deeply painful it will be for the many parents who hope and pray the Lord will turn their children's hearts and heal them from their confusion yet have to say, "But if not…"

Even if they lose custody. Even if their child gets surgery that they may one day regret. Even if their child takes their own life.

Even then, what choice do we have but to remain obedient to God?

On a practical level, we do have a few other things to remember. When the law is pushing for children to learn the ways of the world—ways that not only go against a Christian conscience but also damage a child's psychology regarding sex and sexuality—how should we then respond?

Our only choice is to raise our children with discernment in obedience to the Lord. The reality is, there will always be someone out there who will gladly make themselves available to our children. It is up to parents to ensure that they are the ones their child comes to. And while a parent cannot control their child's mind and heart, we must always be available and make every effort to at least show our children that we are here and we will listen to the questions and struggles they may have.

Our duty, then, is to always point them to Christ—not to morality, not to purity, but to follow Ephesians 4:17-24 in learning Christ. As it says,

> "Now this I say and testify in the Lord, that you must no longer walk as the Gentiles do, in the futility of their minds. They are darkened in their understanding, alienated from the life of God because of the ignorance that is in them, due to their hardness of heart. They have become callous and have given themselves up to sensuality, greedy to practice every kind of impurity. But that is not the way you learned Christ!—assuming that you have heard about him and were taught in him, as the truth is in Jesus, to put off your old self, which belongs to your former manner of life and is corrupt through deceitful desires, and to be renewed in the spirit of your minds, and to put on the new self, created after the likeness of God in true righteousness and holiness."

We bear the likeness of God, and we "learn Christ." He is our salvation, our motivation, and our example. There is nothing else that will capture our hearts the way He has, and we have to show our children the same so that when they are sitting under the heinous, deceptive teachings of the world, they can discern that these things violate God's law.

A House of Welcome

In the Bible, Bethany was a location near Jerusalem frequented by Jesus. Bethany—meaning "a house of welcome"—was truly a town that welcomed Jesus when He stayed with His friends (for a time, anyway).

But in our modern times, Bethany is also the name of a global Christian services organization, which primarily facilitates assistance for adoption, foster care, and pregnancy.

In March 2021, and after a long season of making slow and steady compromises in their U.S.-based fostering programs, Bethany Christian Services is now open to adoptions by same-sex couples.[83]

Their initial compromise under governmental legislation (to require fostering services to same-sex couples) was seen as a difficult choice in which they did not wish to abandon the children they helped. Many have cited that there were other organizations who did not bend to this pressure, but Bethany did. They chose to accept, with seemingly great difficulty, that this was their only option to continue in their work.

But this new decision is different. This was a choice and a declaration that was not made under governmental pressures. It was a culture-based decision. And the culture of Bethany Christian Services no longer lies within biblical Christianity.

---

[83] Shellnutt, K. (2021, March 01). Bethany Christian will Allow LGBT parents to Foster and adopt. Retrieved April 10, 2021, from https://www.christianitytoday.com/news/2021/march/bethany-christian-services-adoption-foster-lgbt-same-sex.html

Person. (2019, November 01). Not giving up on vulnerable kids. Retrieved April 10, 2021, from https://bethany.org/resources/giving-up-not-on-vulnerable-children

The unfortunate consequence of this is that it proves concerns that have been expressed by nations who previously allowed international adoptions. While the adoption system in Ethiopia was in need of drastic reform due to concerns of child trafficking, there were also concerns about those children upon reaching western countries. Some concerns regarded the possibility of abuse or even the tragic death of a child at the hands of her adoptive parents[84] or even the loss of culture. However, another concern was related to the growing prevalence of same-sex couples adopting children.

This particular worry was not widely spoken of in the wake of Ethiopia closing down adoptions. It could easily be assumed that it is because Ethiopia has fairly bad press when it comes to same-sex unions, and they didn't wish to highlight that. But in conversations with many non-diaspora Ethiopians, this is a common theme as to why many were bothered by the prevalence of international adoptions to countries like the U.S.

Bethany Christian Services currently works in Ethiopia, where there are still a significant number of children in need of care and placement as a result of the international adoption shut-down. One cannot help but wonder what the response will be for an organization who has declared wide acceptance of same-sex adoption in a country with a 97% disapproval rating for homosexual lifestyles.[85]

[84] Boiko-Weyrauch, A. (2013, August 20). Adoptive parents on trial in ETHIOPIAN girl's death. Retrieved April 10, 2021, from https://www.seattletimes.com/seattle-news/adoptive-parents-on-trial-in-ethiopian-girlrsquos-death/

[85] Katie J.M. Baker On 12/13/13 at 12:42 PM EST, Dworkin, S., & Kirk, C. (2014, April 22). Ethiopia's war on homosexuals. Retrieved April 10, 2021, from https://www.newsweek.com/ethiopias-war-homosexuals-224457

What will happen to these children now? As Bethany bowed to the U.S. government and cultural pressures, they began to remove themselves from truth. And now, they have walked away from the family structure created by God from the very beginning.

Rendering Unto Caesar

In a previous section, we briefly looked at aspects of Jesus' statement about taxes, but it is important to note is that this was not simply a statement regarding tax law.

For a reminder of the interaction between Jesus and the Pharisees who were trying to trick Him into disobeying the government, here is the exchange:

> But Jesus, aware of their malice, said, "Why put me to the test, you hypocrites? Show me the coin for the tax." And they brought him a denarius. And Jesus said to them, "Whose likeness and inscription is this?" They said, "Caesar's." Then he said to them, "Therefore render to Caesar the things that are Caesar's, and to God the things that are God's." When they heard it, they marveled. And they left him and went away.[86]

The things that bear the likeness of Caesar belong to Caesar. The things that bear the likeness of the world belong to the world. And the things that bear the likeness of God belong to God.

---

[86] Matthew 22:18–22

Our lesson is not only to be in the world and not of it[87] but rather that we are to bear the likeness of God and not give "unto Caesar" what rightly belongs to God. Our devotion is not to the world. Our devotion is to the Lord. So too is our obedience.

We need to emphasize this point. Non-Christians—and worse yet, lukewarm Christians—use this verse to keep Christians from speaking out against the government. "Render unto Caesar what is Caesar's…" I know the popularity as this was one of my go-to verses when I attacked Christians in the past. But, we need to remember this in response and in our hearts: **DO NOT RENDER UNTO CAESAR WHAT IS GOD'S.**

When "Caesar" (i.e. the world system and its governing authorities) demands that we bow to his rule and authority, we can only do so when it does not prevent us from obeying God. We have to maintain the integrity of Scripture even when it is unpopular.

Christian Civil Disobedience is, once more, not an excuse to reject local law. It is a devotion to the truths we are told through the Bible. When we render our obedience to the worldly authorities, we reject the gift of holiness that has set us apart in Christ. If we submit to the muzzle that silences us, and we refrain from proclaiming the truth in Jesus, we not only dishonor God, but we fail in our duty as men and women of the Word who have been given the command to go and make disciples.

Another point made by Thomas Guthrie in light of our duty to proclaim truth, not in defense of God but for the sake of mankind is,

---

[87] A concept derived from Romans 12:2 and Jesus' prayer in John 17:15.

"...this remarkable fact, that God deals with man through the instrumentality of man, communicating by men his will to men."[88]

God first created man, then sent Himself in the likeness of man so that He may proclaim His truth to man and use men to proclaim His truth to other men. If we submit to the men of the world rather than the Son of Man, we render our loyalty and become the likeness of the world.

Learning from the Past

When the laws of our governing authorities violate the law of God, we may always look to those since the Bible who have also battled on these grounds. Unfortunately, we have already seen how these wars are sometimes even fought against church leadership, like in the case of Martin Luther.

It was the law of the church that "indulgences" must be paid. These indulgences were, supposedly, the path for which good, believing Catholics could be rescued from time in Purgatory—a sort of holding-place for the dead who were not bad enough for Hell but not yet good enough to enter Heaven. If they wanted to reach Heaven sooner, or to help their deceased family members to reach Heaven, they had to purchase an indulgence, most of which went toward the building of the elaborate St. Peter's Basilica in Rome.

However, Rome was essentially a theocracy at the time. Emperor Charles V had no choice but to keep Pope Leo X happy. Regardless

---

[88] "The Gospel in Ezekiel" Thomas Guthrie, 1857.

of his own views, he was used as a pawn in efforts to make Luther an outlaw, declaring him just that.

When Luther's supporters staged an abduction in order to protect him, harboring him and keeping him hidden and disguised, Luther was able to continue his work. No matter what the law and the church had declared about him, he was unwilling to give in to the violations of God's law for the sake of his own safety.

And neither did Harriet Tubman.

As an escaped slave who assisted other slaves in escaping, Tubman disobeyed the law of the land to a great extent in the name of justice. She was given the nickname "Moses" for her efforts as an abolitionist prior to the Civil War and as a spy for the Union during the war. Even when the north was subject to laws of returning escaped slaves to their owners, Tubman redirected the Underground Railroad through Canada to preserve the safety of those whom she rescued.[89]

Harriet Tubman was a Christian, and it was her love of deliverance that urged her into many of the duties she enacted. She credited her journey, her health, and her safety to her personal conversations with God. Although she was a supporter of John Brown, an abolitionist who favored violence in gaining freedom for slaves, we can see how Tubman stood firm in her own peaceful efforts to fight against a governing rule that was unjust and unbiblical.

---

[89] Harriet Tubman. (2021, February 26). Retrieved April 10, 2021, from https://www.biography.com/activist/harriet-tubman

Fighting popularity or a populist government—like a corrupt church or lawful slavery—is sometimes required by God.

The Truth of Government and Journalism

There is a lot that comes with discerning whether or not the government is seeking a law which is truly good for us or if it is one which is beneficial only for them, particularly in a country that has often been praised as being the land of the free. Despite having been a blessed or fortunate country for 244 years as of this writing, Christians and citizens of Heaven have to remember one very important thing about humanity: We are sinful people.

Humans are naturally inclined to seek self-serving interests, and we are born to our fleshly nature. This means that just because we believe our nation's leaders have, in the past, sought the prosperity of America's citizens, that doesn't mean that they ever have or ever will seek the good of our souls. Furthermore, it means that it is not paranoia but rather discernment to question the motivations of those in authority.

There is nowhere better to see this than in the relationship between the government and journalism.

In an article from the Harvard Business Review[90], Peter Vanderwicken lays out a case against the honesty and integrity of journalism in western society, exposing it for what it really is: a pawn. He points out that journalists need drama to report, and the

---

[90] Why the news is not the truth. (2014, August 01). Retrieved April 10, 2021, from https://hbr.org/1995/05/why-the-news-is-not-the-truth

government needs reports of drama in order to appear effective in handling said drama. Thus, we are presented with manipulation and lies, leading us to question truth and live in the uncertainty of what we are being told versus what we believe.

This has far-reaching consequences for Christians, who have become excellent fodder for these stories.

If the government wishes to appear devoted to equality and justice, they can easily encourage news reports of "bigoted Christians" whose beliefs prevent them from referring to a person's preferred gender pronoun. This now becomes a major issue as it is spun by the news as being an act of hostility and prejudice against another person.

The media attacked Amy Coney Barrett, questioning her faith as though she could not be impartial for an appeals court seat.[91] This was before the attacks intensified when she was nominated to the Supreme Court.

The Washington Post in reviewing *The Handmaid's Tale* implies that evangelicals are secretly planning this type of future.[92]

ABC has called the Christian non-profit group Alliance for Defending Freedom a hate group.[93]

---

[91] Goodstein, Laurie "Some Worry about Judicial Nominees Ties to a Religious Group." *New York Times* 9-28-2017

[92] Hesse Monica "The Handmaid's Tale has been feared, banned and loved. Now it's scaring the bejeezus out of us again." *Washington Post* April 25 2017. If you read the comments that follow, it is a huge commentary of this assertion. For example, "This book is a vision of the America desired by Christian evangelicals. And they are on their way to making it happen." By bpai_99 4-26-2107 12:14AM

[93] Madden, Pete and Galloway, Erin "Jeff Session addresses 'anti-LGBT hate group,' but DOJ won't release his remarks." ABC News 7-12-2017

CNN's John King questioned the government providing secret service details to family members of the executive branch if they affiliate with faith groups that aren't politically correct.[94]

Unfortunately, this list goes on and on and doesn't even begin to cover the censorship from big tech like Facebook, Twitter, etc...

Now, as a result of this pressure from the media, the government "must act!" They "have to" put a law into place to prove that they are working *for* the people as culture wants them to—as the voters want them to. And what is likely to happen next? A Christian will violate that law, enabling the government to act further by punishing them, on full display for the American people who are already drifting away from the church and toward this brand of "social justice."

But what we can also see in this relationship between the government and the press is how false it is. It both creates and stimulates the viewpoints of the world. It caters to the idea of 'inclusion' while ultimately denying truth of any kind and encouraging others to do so as well. So the narrative drives government, which in turn propagates the narrative. It is an ugly cycle that has western society spinning away from Christian morality at rapid speeds.

Trusting the government to be working for our best interest is unwise. Of course it is good to have hope, and it is good to remain obedient to the law (so long as it is obedient to God's law), but using wisdom to understand when the law goes against what we are taught in the Bible is a vital element of our worship.

---

[94] Hagelin Rebecca "Shame on CNN for attacking Karen Pence's faith." *The Washington Times* 1-20-2019

Whether the government demands that we cease to pray, that we proclaim the Big Bang Theory as absolute truth, or that we decry absolute truth altogether, our only option in the face of violations of God's law is to say, "But if not…"

Daniel prayed with his windows open in faith that God would show him favor for his obedience; but if not, he would have died at the jaws of the lions. Shadrach, Meshach, and Abednego trusted that they would be rescued from the fire; but if not, they would have burned equally with their passion for God. Martin Luther was rescued by his supporters and hidden; but if not, he would have accepted banishment, imprisonment, or execution. Harriet Tubman believed that she would successfully lead people to freedom; but if not, she would have been sent back to her mistress with the knowledge that she had been obedient to God's calling on her life.

All Christians will face their "but if not" moment at some point, and if they are living according to God's will, it will probably happen more than once. It may present itself in romance as, "I hope this person is a believer in Christ; but if not, I will not pursue her." It may present itself in the workplace as, "I hope I will be able to avoid teaching my students to explore their sexual identity; but if not, I am willing to lose my job."

It could even be, "I hope that my country allows me to continue preaching truth from my pulpit; but if not, I will face the consequences and preach truth anyway."

Regardless of what it is and how it presents itself, our likeness should always be that of Jesus as opposed to Caesar; and as we learn

Christ, that likeness should develop further. It is not through the work of obedience that we find salvation, but it is the strength of salvation and the work of Christ that we are enabled to live in obedience to God even when we are told we must not.

CHAPTER SIX:

In Order to Follow God's Commands

WE HAVE ALREADY LOOKED AT TWO WAYS IN WHICH CIVIL disobedience is our duty as a Christian. The first is when we are asked to commit evil. The second one broadens this principle in situations when the laws of the government or society violates God's law. You cannot commit evil without violating God's law, but you can be asked to violate God's law without committing evil.

The third duty a Christian has of civil disobedience is when we must follow God's commands. This one becomes trickier as we have to look at the nuances. It requires a lot of discernment and is harder to explain to others while engaging it. Nevertheless, we have a duty to exercise this discernment in order to follow God's commands. God's commands come in two different places: the Bible (the Word of God) and the Holy Spirit's voice to you in your own heart.

The reason this is trickier is that some of God's commands may be sent only to you. For those fans of the original movie *Blues Brothers*, you may remember as they were trying to get the band back together, Elwood Blues would tell people, "We are on a mission from God."[95] This comedic line was funny, but imagine how it felt if you had to say it to friends and strangers for real.

With that in mind, remember this truth: God may ask you to do something that isn't specifically mentioned in the Bible, but He will never ask you to contradict those Scriptures.

We Cannot but Speak

The account in Acts 4 of Peter and John before the Council, the Sanhedrin, depicts this exact thing. These two men—disciples of Jesus Christ—were preaching to the people when the priests, the temple captain, and the Sadducees came to them and had them arrested. Many people came to know Jesus as a result of these teachings and the miraculous healing of a lame beggar.

When John and Peter were questioned about these teachings and the fact that God had used them as his vessels for a miracle, they boldly declared that the man was healed by the name of Jesus Christ of Nazareth, going on to say that it is the only name under heaven by which we must be saved.[96]

Confused by the healing of this man as the result of two uneducated men, the priests weren't sure what to do about the

---

[95] The *Blue's Brothers* Directed by John Landis. Performances by Dan Akroyd and John Belushi, Universal Pictures 1980
[96] Acts 4:12

ordeal. They didn't want to let them get by with something that was considered heresy, but they also realized they had few options, considering how many people had seen the miracles and thought that John and Peter had been sent by God. The people who had already seen this miracle were going to defend them, and it wouldn't work to try and punish them.

In light of this, the priests and leaders ordered Peter and John not to speak about Jesus anymore. They figured that the best way to get these two men to stop preaching was to simply give them a warning that it wouldn't go well for them if they decided to continue.

But Peter and John were disciples of Jesus—unashamedly. So how did they reply?

> "Whether it is right in the sight of God to listen to
> you rather than to God, you must judge, for we cannot
> but speak of what we have seen and heard."[97]

Although they had been arrested and threatened, John and Peter were unwilling to back down. They could not but speak of what they had seen and heard. Why? The Bible and the "law" did not tell them to speak about Jesus. They received a command from God—the miraculous, merciful God-made-flesh to whom they had dedicated their lives. Silence would be sin.

God had commanded them to declare His name. They couldn't stop. It was their greatest command, and it was one that they

---

[97] Acts 4:19-20

considered an honor, even in the face of great risk, violence, struggle, and ultimately unto death.

Listening for His Voice

There is quite a movement in the Church today regarding letting the Holy Spirit speak to us. While the Holy Spirit is always going to do just that as He leads and guides us in our steps, we have to use extreme discernment to be sure that it is truly the Holy Spirit leading us and not simply our own wants and desires. This is a danger that we see all too often.

What does it look like when we fool ourselves into thinking God is talking just because we want Him to be?

It could be that a very attractive person from work is flattering us—that they are making it evident that they could have an interest in us. As we pray about how to handle this, are we starting to believe that God is opening a door away from our spouse? Could it be that He wants us to pursue this new romance? What if that attractive person attends your church and you both believe strongly in music ministry and your spouse doesn't? Maybe God wants you and this other person to become a husband/wife Christian music sensation!

It's sad how easily we convince ourselves to pursue sin in the name of Christ. Just as we have previously looked at engaging violence for the sake of Christian Civil Disobedience, there are many ways in which we allow ourselves to believe that God will actually be the one leading us down a path that is in direct contrast to His Word.

It is easy as you are reading this to think you cannot be deceived this way. If you are reading this book, I hope you are reading His Book more frequently. Regardless, it is easy to be deceived by your emotions or your flesh, irrespective of your knowledge and relationship with God.

Ravi Zacharias, one of the great apologists, had a way of simply and clearly explaining complex Bible verses and stories, passing down the application to thousands of people. Even he was fooled. Zacharias, after his death, would be exposed in a massive sex scandal that rocked the Christian world. Reports said he would pray with one of the women before they engaged in sex, thanking God for bringing them together.[98]

When I heard this news, it broke my heart. But his deception, sin, and self-delusion do not change any truth he ever spoke from the Word of God—not any more than a cardiologist who smokes two packs of cigarettes a day but tells me not to smoke. I do not mention Zacharias to condemn his clearly condemnable actions but rather to illustrate that if such a knowledgeable man could be taken in by the flesh to break God's law, your knowledge is not sufficient to prevent you from this deception either.

If you think you are hearing from God, verify that it serves His purpose (as revealed in Scripture) and does not contradict it.

As followers of Christ, we know His voice.[99] There is nothing shameful about being a sheep when you have so good a Shepherd.

---

[98] Sillman, Daniel and Shellnutt, Kate, "Ravi Zacharias Hid Hundreds of Pictures of Women, Abuse During Massages, and a Rape Allegation" *Christianity Today* February 11, 2021
[99] John 10:27

One of the most remarkable things about what God has done for us in our lives is that He has allowed us to not only be rescued from our sin, but He has also allowed us to walk with Him in the garden. This means that we truly get to know Him—to be in the midst of His beautiful creation and listen to His voice as He urges us to live in obedience.

We only know His voice if we know *Him*. And knowing God means we must spend time in His Word. We have to discern whether or not the things we believe He is speaking to us are consistent with the clear, evident teachings of His Word.

However, there are also many times when God really will speak to you about matters that may confuse other Christians. They have allowed the world to confuse their understanding of His Kingdom and struggle with the idea that God is speaking to you. This is not only because of potential theological differences but because sometimes the things to which God leads us sound wild and crazy to others.

For instance, let's revisit Harriet Tubman.

Tubman was a strong, bold person who craved justice. However, she also believed that it was the Lord speaking to her as she acted in accordance with that justice.[100] The world tells us that this was the result of a head injury[101] she sustained, which caused her many difficulties in life; but the Holy Spirit *does* speak to us and often leads us to behave in ways that may not make sense to others.

---

[100] Clinton, Catherine *Harriet Tubman: The Road to Freedom* Little Brown and Company 2004 p 93
[101] Ibid, p 38

Just like John and Peter refused to stop speaking about Jesus, Harriet Tubman refused to back down from the work that the Lord had led her to do. From her initial escape to the seemingly illogical paths she would use to lead others to freedom, she consistently claimed that she would go only where the Holy Spirit led her to go as she prayed to God for guidance.[102]

It was listening to His voice that not only gave her the freedom that she had, but also the freedom of so many others. If she had not obeyed, and if she had not known the voice of her Shepherd, she would not have become the woman who has been so historically significant even today.

Another of the many legends who claimed to be led by the Lord is Jeanne D'Arc (Joan of Arc), who led the French army to victory in battle against the English as a nineteen-year-old girl, freeing France from British rule. This took place during one season of the Hundred Years War.

As a young girl, she was extremely devout in her faith. She was profoundly outspoken about her beliefs and about the fact that she received messages from angels who told her to act in accordance with where God led.[103]

Later charged by all pro-English clergymen, Jeanne was declared a heretic[104] and was also charged with cross-dressing as she wore men's clothing in battle and for the sake of preventing assault during seasons when that would be a threat against her. Still, her visions of

---

[102] Ibid p 101
[103] Pernoud, Regine *John of Arc By Herself and Her Witnesses* Scarborough House 1994, 396
[104] Ibid p 3727

angels and claims that God was the one speaking to her and leading her into battle were held by Jeanne until her burning at the stake.[105] Legend says that her heart never burned.[106]

Did Harriet Tubman and Joan of Arc hear from the Lord? Was it really the Holy Spirit that led them into the dangerous situations in which they found themselves? I do not see a reason to doubt them. The book of Acts records multiple incidents in which the Holy Spirit guided people. However, that isn't something that we can ever know for certain this side of Heaven, but what we do see is that their actions and their bravery, which they declared a result of obedience to the Holy Spirit, saved many lives and brought great freedom and victory—even at personal cost. (To see a list of the ways the Holy Spirit manifested in Acts, refer to Appendix A).

As with Tubman and Joan of Arc, the world will not always see it this way when we obey the Lord, but that isn't up to us. Whether we lose friends, position, or even our very lives, we are to follow Him out of obedience.

The Holy Spirit only asks us to do things that will align with God's Word, but frequently these things will not align with our worldly wants and desires. Still, we are called to follow. No matter how frightening it might be, not only might we need to reject the laws of the world but sometimes even the things the world declares "wise."

---

[105] Ibid 4231
[106] Ibid 4287

1 Corinthians 4:10 says, "We are fools for Christ's sake, but you are wise in Christ. We are weak, but you are strong. You are held in honor, but we in disrepute."

Romans 1:22 says, "Professing themselves to be wise, they became fools."

It's alright if we are considered fools because, ultimately, we are fools for Christ. Where we are weak, He is strong. And where our reputations are lacking, He remains the King of Kings.

Following Like Paul

There are few heroes of the New Testament who strike us as much as Paul. This man was devout in his hatred of Christians. He was a firm believer of the ruling party of Jews who believed that Jesus was a blasphemer and liar.

However, Paul met Jesus, the risen Christ, on the road to Damascus. In Acts 9, it says,

> But Saul, still breathing threats and murder against the disciples of the Lord, went to the high priest and asked him for letters to the synagogues at Damascus, so that if he found any belonging to the Way, men or women, he might bring them bound to Jerusalem.
>
> Now as he went on his way, he approached Damascus, and suddenly a light from heaven shone around him. And falling to the ground, he heard a voice saying to him, "Saul, Saul, why are you persecuting me?"

And he said, "Who are you, Lord?" And he said, "I am Jesus, whom you are persecuting. But rise and enter the city, and you will be told what you are to do." The men who were traveling with him stood speechless, hearing the voice but seeing no one. Saul rose from the ground, and although his eyes were opened, he saw nothing. So they led him by the hand and brought him into Damascus.[107]

Paul was hunting Christians before he met Christ. But instantly, when Jesus spoke to him, Paul knew who he was and called him, "Lord."

As a diligent believer in God, Paul had learned to heed the voice of God and discovered that, in Jesus, he heard that voice. He knew exactly to whom he belonged and that this man was God made flesh.

This would have been a complete shock to Paul's community. His friends and the others in leadership positions would have been terribly upset by his sudden turnaround, his decision to follow Jesus. He was becoming the very thing they all hated—he most zealously of them all.

Imagine a zealous atheist in modern times, such as Richard Dawkins—a man who verbally attacks and attempts to discredit Christians—suddenly throwing himself at the foot of the cross. While he doesn't publicly execute Christians (like Paul), he works to do whatever harm he is able in an effort to prove us fools. And if he

---

[107] Acts 9:1–8

turned to Jesus? He would lose everything! His life's work—the thing he is the most known for—would be worthless. He would lose his friends. People would think he had lost his mind.

So to move from persecuting Christians to advocating for Christians would be unheard of and only a miracle—not to mention, actually becoming one of those Christians himself.

And yet, Paul suddenly understood that it was worth it. He was willing to give up everything now that he had been called by Jesus. To do anything but serve Him would have been impossible.

Then we see that Jesus commanded Paul to do another unthinkable task.

He was called not to reach the Jews, as would be at least somewhat acceptable for him. Instead he was called to go to the Gentiles (non-Jews) to proclaim that even *they* could be among God's chosen people.

For the most part, aside from a few exceptions, the majority of Christians at the time came from among the Jews. For a Jew in Paul's position to consort with Gentiles was unthinkable.

Now they had the gift of grace available to them, and Paul was the one charged with bringing that Word. Paul didn't just give up his comfort by becoming a Christian, he was forced into the unthinkable of reaching out to the Gentiles and proclaiming the Word of God to them.

There may be times when, on the surface, if feels as though God is asking us to do the impossible. And there are times when He really will be asking us to do the impossible. The idea that *God will not give us more than we can handle* is a misunderstood and misquoted claim based on 1 Corinthians 10:13, which says, "No temptation has overtaken you that is not common to man. God is faithful, and he will not let you be tempted beyond your ability, but with the temptation he will also provide the way of escape, that you may be able to endure it."

In reality, God often gives us more than we can bear. If He didn't, why would we even need Him? If we could do all things in our own strength, if we could bear all things just by trying extra hard, there would be no need for God, and there would be no glory for Him in the end.

Nevertheless, God often allows us to succeed in His mission and call for our lives and for those around us. Whether we see great victory or the task is more than we can bear, He is our strength, and He will provide a way even in the midst of our struggles.

A Tale of Trust[108]

It was in the 1920's when a woman felt the call, through a series of images, to give her life to Jesus and move overseas, risking everything. She accepted.

Lydia Prince moved to Jerusalem with $200. She was unable to work due to her foreign status. She had no other means of supporting herself and had to live each day with faith that God would provide for her, just as He had called her to go.

---

[108] Prince, Derek and Prince, Lydia, *Appointment in Jerusalem: A True Story of Faith, Love, and the Miraculous Power of Prayer* Whitaker House 2013

During this volatile time, and as one of the few and unfavored Christians, Lydia found herself caught in the conflict of Arabs and Jews.

Even when she was already living day to day, trusting that God would not abandon her, a starving baby was left with her to take care of. Lydia, having no sustenance even for herself, was tasked with finding milk and food for the little one. We can only imagine how we might respond in such an instance, but Lydia had no intention of abandoning the child, even at personal cost.

She depended, fully, on the Lord for provision. Lydia knew that God would not have sent her to Jerusalem without reason, and she had to put her complete trust in His hands. In the midst of it all, she experienced struggles and victories but also supernatural help from God. This led her to running an orphanage for Jewish and Arab children, regardless of the fact that these two groups were never supposed to mingle. Among those children, she ultimately adopted nine daughters.

Eventually, a young, British soldier, twenty-five years younger than Lydia, came into her life. His name was Derek Prince, and he soon married Lydia. Inspired by her selflessness and faith, they began Derek Prince Ministries, a ministry which has survived both of them and is now global and thriving.

Many people would have considered Lydia to be foolish for the journey she undertook, but God has used that obedience to do amazing things. From her care for the orphaned children in her community to the resulting ministry, her influence has impacted thousands.

Know His Voice

There is an old story that has been told in different forms, but we will go with the version of a group of pilgrims who wanted to visit the Holy Land. While touring on a bright and beautiful day, they were making their way through the streets until they found an establishment where they could order some food. As they sat and ate, they suddenly heard the sound of screams coming from down the road.

Distressed by the sound, the pilgrims turned and looked, trying to discern what was happening. There were hundreds of shrill wails and cries coming ever closer.

What they saw was a herd of sheep being driven by an angry man with a whip. He snapped it when they were too slow, driving them with great ferocity. He was cruel to his sheep, treating them terribly in a harsh display.

The pilgrims were shocked and upset. They had never seen a shepherd be so cruel to his sheep. Moreover, they had never heard sheep scream like that. It was painfully disturbing to see not only his mean behavior toward the sheep, but also how the sheep lived in terror.

The waiter came by to bring the pilgrims more bread and could see that they were distressed. Upon his asking them if they were all right, they explained what was bothering them—that they had never before seen a shepherd treat his sheep so cruelly.

The waiter shook his head and looked at the pilgrims in earnest before explaining, "That's not the shepherd. That's the butcher."

As sheep, we know who leads us, and we know who leads us to our deaths. They are two very different tasks. But wherever the Shepherd leads, even through a storm and terror, we can trust Him. Where the butcher leads, even through a beautiful city on a sunny day, we cannot place our faith in the pleasant circumstances. The end is death.

It is possible that the Lord will supernaturally, through His Holy Spirit, ask you to engage in Civil Disobedience. It is important that we are prepared for that to happen because it will require boldness and certainty in our faith.

As we keep our minds open to the possibility of God calling us to Civil Disobedience, we can't put Him in a box and assume that He is only going to ask us to do the easy things or the things that make us comfortable. The fact is, sometimes He does lead His people to do things that don't make sense at the time—things that make us uncomfortable.

If and when He does, we have to hold fast to our faith and obedience that He is the one who leads us and it's not up to us to decide what will bring God glory. He may be glorified by rescuing us from the flames like Shadrach, Meshach, and Abednego, "but if not"—if He is glorified by rescuing France and then we are burned at the stake—we still must honor His calling.

Because God is unchangeable and He cannot lie, we know that His leading will not contradict His Word. If God calls us to Civil Disobedience, it will never be to act out of hatred or fear. It is a calling to trust Him, and Christian Civil Disobedience is not disobedience to God.

If you believe that He is calling you to something that does contradict His Word, it is best to seek spiritual counsel from a solid leader in the faith, or multiple if you fear that your preferred leader could have similar biases to you that would lead them to approve without seeking God first. But, ultimately, seek the Word and see if you really do stand in contradiction with it. If so, you have your answer.

We must stop complicating how we hear His voice. His sheep know His voice, and we are those sheep. We should always know when our Shepherd is speaking. His Word is true and timeless—the same yesterday, today, and forever.

Spend time in the Word. Trust it. It will not steer you wrong.

CHAPTER SEVEN:

Rooted in the Fear of God and Not Human Anger

THERE ARE INDEED TIMES WHEN IT IS PERMISSIBLE TO ENGAGE THE act of Christian Civil Disobedience, but that is not the only thing we need to focus on. Behind every decision we make, we have a motivation and a reason.

Because of this, we have to cautiously pay attention to the reasons we have for employing this response. We have to ask ourselves, even if it is uncomfortable and interferes with our justifying, why exactly are we behaving the way we are?

Typically, we will find that we are responding with Civil Disobedience for one of two reasons. The first is that the situation is an offense to *God*. The second is that we are angry because something has offended *me*.

If our anger is rooted in frustrated offense against ourselves, we know in our heads how we ought to respond. Getting our hearts to comply may be more difficult, but through prayer and seeking the

Lord we may be able to let go of whatever anger and bitterness dwells within us. As long as we are willing to let go of the mentality that we are just being ourselves and out for our own good, we can live according to the law of God and in the humility of Scripture.

In a world that is ever-increasingly self-focused, while personal responsibility is removed in order to live under a pretense of being "socially" focused, we have to decide how much freedom of interpretation is allowed in truth before we have drifted further into our own self-defense as opposed to having a ready defense of the Gospel in hand. And while, as we remember, we are not needed by God to defend *Him*, this defense should always be done in order that others might see and know Him in all His glory.

The problem arises when we are angry purely on our own behalf under a guise of spirituality. I experienced this a lot when I would try to aggravate Christians. My favorite go-to was evolution and the definition of the first seven days. I used every linguistic argument to twist and turn the Bible to mask and confuse the arguments. Further, I attacked the arguments using carbon dating.

I remember one Christian who showed me a video that mentions potential inconsistencies with carbon dating, arguments for intelligent design, theories from a Christian perspective that can explain away all signs of evolution in the earth. Regardless, all of the intellectual arguments were fruitless against me.

Other atheists of the day will also not budge. They adamantly declare that the world is not one of order, but of chaos. It is too fragile. People are too fragile. Furthermore, it doesn't make sense for there to be some invisible deity out there.

Regardless of whether it was me "before Christ" or a present-day atheist, the reaction is frequently the same: the Christian begins to get frustrated. They say that none of this could have existed without a Creator. At which point, the aggravator retorts that the Creator must also have been created.

The circular debate continues on. My goal was to aggravate the Christian and point out all the flaws. It didn't matter if I won or lost the debate, I was trying to make the Christian lose the debate. And, if I made them cry in the process, that was bonus points in my book—something that I could brag about like a medal to my intelligent friends.

But for the average Christian, to debate logically as opposed to spiritually, the arguments may blur and become frustrating.[109] With most debates, there are nuances that must be handled delicately. Christians too often shift their attention away from changing hearts and toward winning the argument at any cost. After all, it is for the sake of God, isn't it? Isn't it all for His glory that the Christian should find an opportunity to not only challenge, but occasionally mock the atheist if they talk themselves in a circle?

Unfortunately, without realizing it, this happens all too often in how we address the world with Christianity. Instead of holding fast to the devotion to glorify God, we begin to drift into the arena of

---

[109] To watch a great debate where a Christian rarely gets frustrated with any of these tactics, I highly recommend the debate between John Lennox and Peter Atkins. Unbelievable. "Lennox vs. Atkins – Can Science explain everything? (Official Debate Video)" YouTube 17 February 2019 https://www.youtube.com/watch?v=fSYwCaFkYno

wanting to be right, wanting to be justified before our peers, and wanting to be *known* for our devotion rather than *being* devoted.

More often than not, the Christian I was aggravating ended up trying to mock me in return, yell at me, or storm off in a childlike rant. I even had a pastor threaten to fight me, and another kicked me out of his office!

Once you lose sight of God and your pride kicks in, more often than not, this gives way to anger; and your poor reaction to your anger does not please God.

I cannot emphasize this enough: We are here to share the gospel through our Civil Disobedience. We are showing people who Christ is through us, not how smart we are or how persuasive our speech may be.

Be Quick; Be Slow

In James 1:19-20, we are told, "Know this, my beloved brothers: let every person be quick to hear, slow to speak, slow to anger; for the anger of man does not produce the righteousness of God."

We may have heard as children that there was a reason God designed us with two ears and only one mouth. (Perhaps this could even be our evidence of intelligent design in our future debates!) We are far better off listening twice as much as we speak. If we hear before adding our own thoughts, we might have a more complete understanding.

This is very often the case. And when responding to pressures against our faith, we have a choice to make in how much we intend to listen to others and how much we are going to speak on our own behalf. What we may find is that a good portion of our disagreements are merely the result of a lack of understanding. Even if we are in the right and the other party is in the wrong, if we listen first, we can have a better understanding of their reasoning.

A recent example of this is how many churches shut down during the COVID-19 pandemic as a result of their Governor's orders.

We already looked at our responsibility to meet together and that the Bible gives us no provisions for pandemics—although we do have a personal responsibility to the body of Christ (called "love") to not knowingly infect others and put them at risk—and we can understand that there were a lot of different views on this even from within the Christian community. Although we may feel we had a very valid point, we cannot address others without hearing their valid points as well.

For those who believed that it was entirely irresponsible to leave home and that social responsibility to our fellow Christians meant watching church online, listening closely to reasons for attending church anyway from those who chose to do so could have been very difficult. Without listening to the reasons, it may have seemed that those Christians were being brash and uncaring, reckless and unhinged about something they were not experts in.

And for those Christians who believed that meeting together on Sundays was imperative for those who were not clearly infected, the Christians who stayed at home would have sounded like cowards or sheep who disregarded certain aspects of Scripture.

Chances are, even after listening to the arguments of the other side, no one changed their mind. However, when we pause to listen to the arguments, we can at least have a respectful dialogue without attacking the other as "uncaring" or "cowardly." And when these arguments are not within the Church but are being fought against the world, we need to be just as cautious to understand why the world argues for things we deem so ugly and sinful. We have to understand the sin that is behind those arguments.

We have to understand the sin behind "population control" when the government puts provisions in place to restrict how many children we can have—especially when the very first mandate God gave to us is to be fruitful and multiply.[110] We have to listen as they talk about the impacts of too many people on the world, and we have to consider those arguments before throwing out our own.

Whatever a person believes about the politicized aspects of the climate and earth, God did also tell us to subdue the earth. He gave us stewardship over it. So, as we seek to take care of the world in a responsible way and not neglect it, we can bear this perspective in mind for those who are angry at us for believing in God's mandate to multiply. Even if we disagree, we can find the common ground if we will simply listen.

Unfortunately, we should never expect the same dignity returned to us. As we listen to the reasoning of others who put restrictions on us that may violate our consciences, we cannot expect those people to hear us out in reply. Even if the mother of eight children is an eco-

---

[110] Genesis 1:28

friendly, vegetarian homesteader who makes a side income selling compost from food waste in a package made from recycled bottles she gathered while diving in an ocean cleanup, she is unlikely to be heard. Even if we honor this world that God gave us and treat it with utmost respect, we cannot expect tolerance if the law begins to shift in a way that limits our freedom to have more children[111].

This example is certainly reflective of the infamous "one-child policy" in China[112], which now allows two children but is also an ideology being spread in popular culture and by some of the world's loudest voices, including population-control-enthusiast Bill Gates, whose father sat on the board of Planned Parenthood[113] and who has given many talks on his theories of using vaccines as a means of population control[114].

The point of these intricate examples is not to focus on the debate, however. It is understanding sin. It is understanding the sin of authorities who force us to do something against our conscience, and it is understanding our own sinful tendencies and discerning how to respond righteously. There may be times when someone we

---

[111] Follett, C., About the Author Chelsea Follett, Chelsea Follett Policy Analyst and Managing Editor of HumanProgress.Org, & Policy Analyst and Managing Editor of HumanProgress.Org. (2021, January 22). Politicians' support for population control is dangerous. Retrieved April 10, 2021, from https://www.cato.org/commentary/politicians-support-population-control-dangerous

[112] One-child policy. (n.d.). Retrieved April 10, 2021, from https://www.britannica.com/topic/one-child-policy

[113] Stuart Glascock | Photos by Dan LaMont | June 2013 issue. (n.d.). The immense impact of Bill Gates Sr. Retrieved April 10, 2021, from https://magazine.washington.edu/feature/the-immense-impact-of-bill-gates-sr/

[114] Gates, who, and Abortion vaccines. (2020, July 18). Retrieved April 10, 2021, from https://fcpp.org/2020/07/19/gates-who-and-abortion-vaccines/

Fredrick Nzwili | Religion News Service. (2014, November 11). Kenya's Catholic BISHOPS: TETANUS vaccine is birth control in disguise. Retrieved April 10, 2021, from https://www.washingtonpost.com/national/religion/kenyas-catholic-bishops-tetanus-vaccine-is-birth-control-in-disguise/2014/11/11/3ece10ce-69ce-11e4-bafd-6598192a448d_story.html

disagree with has a very valid point. Their concern may be perfectly legitimate. But if that concern goes against the law of God, even the law which has been fulfilled in Christ, we have no choice but to turn our backs on it and choose to follow Jesus.

Revisiting Shiphrah and Puah

In a previous chapter, we looked at the midwives of Moses' time who refused to murder the Hebrew baby boys. These two brave souls may serve as an excellent reminder to us for the way we ought to respond when we are faced with the decision to engage in civil disobedience.

How did they respond? In Exodus 1:17, it says, "But the midwives feared God and did not do as the king of Egypt commanded them, but let the male children live."

These two women made the right decision to uphold God's law and to let these boys live. They made a firm decision to obey Him.

But why? Was it out of their own anger? Were they sitting there, furious about the fact that they were meant to kill the boys born of their own people? In all honesty, they probably were. But what was their reason for disobeying? We read exactly what it says, *"But the midwives feared God…"*

They were not brave in their own strength. They were brave because of their fear of the Lord. Nothing else could lead them into a place of bravery like this. But they feared God enough to live obediently to Him.

If we compare this with our modern infanticide and look at how Christians respond to abortion, there is a very real risk that we are not fighting abortion with the same motivations used by Shiphrah and Puah.

When we look at the modern pro-life movement, we often see it posed as a human rights issue. This isn't deniable by any means, but even this human rights violation—even murder—should not be our primary calling in fighting this heinous act. We may absolutely recognize that it is a justice issue and that it is a genocide, but even that is not what our primary motivator should be.

Our motivation to any kind of dissent against the world and culture should always be upon the basis of fearing God. There is no other factor so important as this. There is no other reason for us to give up our lives or to disobey the world around us. Our only worthwhile reason for Civil Disobedience as Christians is the fear of the Lord.

Be Angry and Do Not Sin

It is made very clear to us in Ephesians 4:26-27 how we ought to behave in moments of anger.

> "Be angry and do not sin; do not let the sun go down on your anger, and give no opportunity to the devil."

So what does this mean for us? It means that our anger must be for righteousness' sake. Even the verse quoted earlier in James 1:19–20 does not say anger is disallowed but rather that we should be "slow to anger."

The Bible, in this passage and in its context, is actually telling us to "be angry." It is not saying to push aside our anger or to pretend that it doesn't exist. Instead, it's telling us there are parameters within which to actually engage that anger.[115]

However, we are not to *sin* in our anger. There are still restrictions on how we behave. How we enact our anger must display the holiness of God.

We also read that we are not to let the sun go down on our wrath or give the devil a foothold. While this could refer to an exact period of time—as in allowing yourself to be angry for a day but not holding onto it for the next—we can also interpret this as a warning against bitterness.

Once we allow bitterness to take root in our lives, that is the harvest we will eventually produce. The warning against lingering in our anger is one to remind us that we cannot hold fast to things which will inevitably make us hard.

Bitterness in marriage or family relationships are frequently spoken of. People go to therapy for it all the time. People deal with anger against loved ones because of past hurts or even little things. A

---

[115] Before you think that I am talking about "righteous anger," notice that the Bible never references the term righteous anger. This is a human constructed term to justify your anger. The Bible does give parameters to your anger, but it does not carte blanche allow for "righteous anger." For example, it does not say, "Do not be angry unless your anger is righteous." For a great word study, look up anger in the Bible and see when it is allowed and when it is not.

wife may be bitter about her husband's past affair or she may be bitter because he repeatedly turns down the thermostat in the winter. Whether something big or small, this can be an impactful burden to carry.

However, when we look at bitterness and the sun going down on our wrath, we can see it in a greater context as well. We can look at it in a political or cultural format to see that bitterness and anger, when left to linger, are an ugly thing indeed.

Take, for instance, the current cultural climate in America. There is bitterness from the younger generation over the older generation's prosperity. There is bitterness between races. There is bitterness against the church for not affirming all lifestyles as holy.

What we have to be wary of as Christians is recognizing that bitterness can breed more bitterness. If we are on the receiving end of someone else's wrath and bitterness, it is very possible that we might return it. After all, we deserve justification from their anger, don't we?

Well, according to the Bible, if we let the sun go down on our wrath and we give in to this bitterness, we are giving the devil a foothold in our lives. These things only lead to hate, and if the first and second commandments are to love God and to love our neighbors, hate is the very antithesis of how we are to live.

So what does it look like when we are up against someone else's evil? Are we not allowed to respond in anger against the things of this world that contradict God? Of course we are! But our anger must be tempered. God is full of wrath for sin, but He is full of mercy for the repentant. What we must do with our own lives is to root our fear in the Lord as opposed to human anger. If an issue violates our conscience on Christian terms, seeking God's guidance and wisdom with the issue is the primary need. From there, we too must be merciful for those who repent.

Jesus gives us a great reminder in the parable of the tares.

> Another parable He put forth to them, saying: "The kingdom of heaven is like a man who sowed good seed in his field; but while men slept, his enemy came and sowed tares among the wheat and went his way. But when the grain had sprouted and produced a crop, then the tares also appeared. So the servants of the owner came and said to him, 'Sir, did you not sow good seed in your field? How then does it have tares?' He said to them, 'An enemy has done this.' The servants said to him, 'Do you want us then to go and gather them up?' But he said, 'No, lest while you gather up the tares you also uproot the wheat with them. Let both grow together until the harvest, and at the time of harvest I will say to the reapers, 'First gather together the tares and bind them in bundles to burn them, but gather the wheat into my barn.'"[116]

---

[116] Matthew 13:24–30, NKJV

He further explained this parable to the disciples:

> "He who sows the good seed is the Son of Man. The field is the world, the good seeds are the sons of the kingdom, but the tares are the sons of the wicked *one*. The enemy who sowed them is the devil, the harvest is the end of the age, and the reapers are the angels. Therefore as the tares are gathered and burned in the fire, so it will be at the end of this age. The Son of Man will send out His angels, and they will gather out of His kingdom all things that offend, and those who practice lawlessness, and will cast them into the furnace of fire. There will be wailing and gnashing of teeth."[117]

The wheat and the tares may look similar, but at the end, Jesus will send His angels to destroy the imposters. When we engage with non-Christians in anger, we feel like *we* must remove the tares, but that is not our responsibility. Our responsibility is to be the wheat and trust Him to remove the tares when the time is right.

---

[117] Matthew 13:38–42, NKJV

CHAPTER EIGHT

Done for Saving Lives and Not Destroying Lives

OUR CIVIL DISOBEDIENCE MUST HAVE INTENT BEHIND IT. THERE will always be motivations for our actions, and it is up to us to decide what those are. But after the motivations, we have to also look at the *goal* of our decision to enact Civil Disobedience as a Christian.

What outcome are we trying to achieve? Will the intention be for the sake of saving others? Or will it be the destruction of others? What do we ultimately hope to achieve as a result of our actions?

It is important that, when we look at these questions, we recognize that our efforts can't be focused on rising up against our foes but rather seeing the people of the world draw near to Christ. If we separate our morality from righteousness, we end up with the type of anger and bitterness we already looked at.

Motivations and goals are two separate things, but they should be intertwined. Apart from God, our motivation could be social justice and our goal could be seeing people protected.

With God, our motivation should be to love our neighbor and our goal should be to see souls come to Christ as a result of that love.

These distinctions get muddied. Oftentimes, we are so distracted by the physical, earthly presence of justice issues that we completely forget about the heavenly aspect, and that is a far more important thing for us to focus on.

Because we have looked at the importance of nonviolence and reaching others with love, we can look at some more specific examples as to how these translate into our ultimate goals as people of God who are seeking to bring peace to the world, but who are also focused on bringing the world to Christ and showing how His love is the greatest thing yet to come.

There are warnings in the Bible to prepare us for these times, which is why it is so important that we look at the issue of Civil Disobedience and prepare our hearts for the day we need to take a stand. Among those warnings is Matthew 24:6, where we read, "And you will hear of wars and rumors of wars. See that you are not alarmed, for this must take place, but the end is not yet."

In the context of this verse, Jesus is talking about the signs of the End of the Age. There are so many aspects of this to look at, but aside from the Eschatological points—which can be debated all day long since the Bible tells us that we will *not know* the day or the hour no matter how much decoding we try to do—we can see the very present point that a part of our life on this earth prior to the coming of Christ is that people will rise against people.

If the first greatest commandment is to love God and the second greatest commandment is to love our neighbor[118], we can be confident that the greatest temptation will be to worship something else as our god, and the second greatest temptation will be to despise our neighbors and to put our own desires above theirs, making no sacrifices of ourselves but creating an insular world in which we are more important than they are.

This is very important to repeat as we have to be careful to not fall into a worldly trap.

Again: We can be confident that the greatest temptation will be to worship something else as our god, and the second greatest temptation will be to despise our neighbors and to put our own desires above theirs.

This has played out around the globe through genocides, slavery, unjust immigration laws (as opposed to the legitimate immigration laws), and even down to simple land disputes between neighbors who want an extra foot of lawn. From the cruelest of hatreds to the pettiest of wants, human nature says that we are more important than others and that it is *our own* life which must be bettered.

I wish I could tell you that I have held myself higher than petty disputes, but I have fallen into this trap many times. I have learned, though, to watch myself and guard against doing that.

The Christian view, in contrast, shows that our actions must be made in order to bless others and grant them the grace and mercy that we have been granted.

---

[118] Matthew 22:34-40

Racial Injustices and Responses

If we look again at the Rodney King riots of 1992, we see people who were deeply broken by an oppressive system and rose up in response. But were they responding to better the lives of their own community? Or was it about making a statement against those who had first pushed them down?

Unfortunately, this violent act did not give them the ultimate outcome they might have wanted. Rather than an improved community with better economic focus and stronger unity, the riots have gone down in history for chaos, destruction, and a failure to create any significant change. And even if they were justified, many members of the community had to pay the consequences of those actions.

What we have to ask is whose lives were on the line? Were these protests carried out in order to save lives or to destroy them? Were people bettered by the protests or did they, on the whole, have a negative impact?

Unfortunately, the people of the community were the ones who had to dramatically pay the price. Their lives were on the line and their lives were not 'saved' by these actions. Thousands were injured, thousands were arrested, and the community was left no better off than it had been previously.

This was an uprising of anger against corruption, not a fight against corruption in order to actually save lives, whether that be physical, spiritual, emotional, to financial. From the LA Four[119] to looters and petty thieves, the community was torn apart not only by the oppressive police system and the strikingly poor economy, but by the fury of those who chose to engage in violent measures.

Without contrast, the August 2017 White Lives Matter protests in Charlottesville, Virginia, were deeply ugly. Although it looked different and these protests were organized and systematic, that did not stop the chaos from erupting as the white supremacists who led the charge tried to make their own statements about race.

The White Lives Matter protest was deeply shameful in its goals to elevate the status of whites and devalue those of other races. Instead of seeing all mankind created in God's image, these protestors wanted to see to it that their so-called "superior" race remained in charge. It was a declaration that they deemed their own lives as more valuable than other races and, in the end, resulted in a murder, two accidental deaths, and at least thirty-three nonfatal injuries[120].

Heather Heyer was the young woman who died in the incident when James Alex Fields Jr. intentionally plowed his car into a group of counter-protestors. In addition, the ramming left at least twenty-eight others injured, leaving us to realize just how ugly human nature can be outside of Christ. Of course, there are many who do such things in His name, with hearts that are made of flesh and don't even realize it.

---

[119] A group of four men who were charged with multiple assaults during the riots, including a horrific beating.
[120] ABC news. (n.d.). Retrieved April 12, 2021, from https://abcnews.go.com/US/happen-charlottesville-protest-anniversary-weekend/story?id=57107500

These protests were certainly not about saving white lives. In fact, Heather Heyer was a white woman, so if that had been anyone's goal, they were certainly failures. But this victim mindset led to a display in which no one's lives were bettered, and anyone with a sense of justice could see that it was sheer lunacy.

While most people can see that the death of a black woman would have been equally tragic and criminal, the actual outcome that happened is evidence that James Alex Fields Jr. and the others alongside him didn't care about saving anyone's life. They were mindlessly bent on destruction, even to the consequence of a life they deem superior.

Both the LA Riots and the White Lives Matter riots showed the consequence of fighting in order to make a point of anger rather than a stand against injustice through the love of Christ. They did not achieve their intended goal, but rather left communities devastated.

But when we look at these events in contrast to the work of Martin Luther King Jr. and those who fought peacefully in the Civil Rights Movement, it is painfully clear that there is a right way to handle injustice as opposed to the wrong ways seen above.

Martin Luther King fought back through peaceful methods. However, just because they were peaceful doesn't mean they were easy. In fact, it may have been easier if he had thrown his weight around or enacted violence that would force the government to appease him just to get things to stop.

As a result of his actions, Martin Luther King Jr. was imprisoned and, ultimately, assassinated. As with all men, King had flaws, but regardless of these shortcomings, it does not negate the incredible stand he took to fight for the equality of all races and peoples within the United States and how those effects have been seen internationally for the ultimate good of many people.

But this is where we return to the real change we want to see. If we are looking for an external change, yes, we can behave however we wish, and we might see policies shift or hear authorities making promises to us that they never intend to keep. But heart changes? That is something we will scarcely see as a result of loud, angry measures.

This is why Martin Luther King Jr. is a name that has been made famous, whereas so many of the anarchists of the time are less well-known and are spoken of with derision when mentioned at all.

The Bible and Race

Of course, as with all issues of justice, we need to look at what Scripture tells us about this issue. What does the Bible have to say about race?

Many people point to the Bible as being a defender of slavery and a proponent of segregation. While there are a great many contextual aspects to this, what we do see is that God is not a God of senseless discrimination. Instead, the Bible is clear that God has His chosen people, but all men are created in His image.

Salvation, once set apart for a specific race and people—although there were those brought into the fold such as Ruth and Rahab—has been offered once for all[121], and there are ample New Testament samples of this, which reflect the same loving God of the Old Testament. As Christians, we need to know that we act with reason when we stand firm against injustice, and that begins by acknowledging what the Bible has to say on an issue.

In Galatians 3:28, we read, "There is neither Jew nor Greek, there is neither slave nor free, there is no male and female, for you are all one in Christ Jesus."

Acts 10:34-35 says, "So Peter opened his mouth and said: 'Truly I understand that God shows no partiality, but in every nation anyone who fears him and does what is right is acceptable to him.'"

James 2:8-9 tells us, "If you really fulfill the royal law according to the Scripture, 'You shall love your neighbor as yourself,' you are doing well. But if you show partiality, you are committing sin and are convicted by the law as transgressors."

And in Revelation 7:9–10, it says, "After this I looked, and behold, a great multitude that no one could number, from every nation, from all tribes and peoples and languages, standing before the throne and before the Lamb, clothed in white robes, with palm branches in their hands, and crying out with a loud voice, 'Salvation belongs to our God who sits on the throne, and to the Lamb!'"

These are just a mere few select verses that show us the diversity of God's Kingdom. This is, of course, aside from the account of creation wherein God made man in His image. Not *some* men. Man. As in, all men. Or, perhaps more clearly, "mankind."

---

[121] Romans 1:16, John 3:16–18, 1 Timothy 2:4; 2 Peter 3:9; 1 John 2:2

Since the Bible is in support of all people and all races being welcomed into the family of God, it is absolutely a necessity as Christians that we stand firm in the belief that all life is intrinsically valuable. But when we take this stand, we should also remember that ultimate goal we have.

Our moral obligations mean nothing if separated from the glory of God and the commitment to worshiping Him. If we are not devoted to that as our primary goal, there is little that we can do to make a real difference.

The Great Commission and Our Duty

Throughout history we have seen that not everyone who takes a stand in a peaceful, moral manner is a Christian, but there truly should be a correlation between moral dealings in the face of conflict and those who claim to be followers of Christ.

As Christians, when we see injustice, it is not our duty to be loud, nor is it our duty to be heard. It *is*, however, our duty to speak. Remaining silent is not always equal to being complicit, but there are many times when a mainstream message may have the misfortune of being both true and also deeply flawed. This happens when a legitimate issue of justice is clouded by political goals or ideologies. As Christians wishing to avoid certain politics, we don't necessarily have the luxury of staying silent, but we may have to make the choice to speak a message parallel to, yet varied from, that mainstream message.

For instance, there are many Christians who support the idea that black lives matter, but they do not support the organization of the same name due to its political ties. That doesn't mean that these Christians ought to remain silent in the face of injustice. The same can be said for Christians who wish to fight human trafficking but find that they can't support certain organizations who provide abortions for women who have been rescued from sex slavery.

As Christians, we do not have the luxury of staying silent, nor do we have the luxury of abandoning all self-restraint and throwing ourselves into anger against an issue. Instead, we have a clear and focused goal with which to align.

That goal can be found in Matthew 28:16-20.

> "Now the eleven disciples went to Galilee, to the mountain to which Jesus had directed them. And when they saw him they worshiped him, but some doubted. And Jesus came and said to them, 'All authority in heaven and on earth has been given to me. Go therefore and make disciples of all nations, baptizing them in the name of the Father and of the Son and of the Holy Spirit, teaching them to observe all that I have commanded you. And behold, I am with you always, to the end of the age.'"

We have been called to follow the Great Commission. Any issue we choose to stand against must be in line with that, just as our response must be in line with it. Nothing in our actions can or should detract from the Great Commission to which we have been called.

Just as God has given us grace to overcome sin on our behalf, He gives us wisdom through the Holy Spirit to guide us into right actions, right choices, and right words. In light of this, our responses should always be levied against whether or not they are in line with the Great Commission.

Will our Civil Disobedience take us where we need to go? Will it lead us to making disciples? Will we represent a Gospel that is petty and bitter? Or will we show the world a Gospel rich in mercy, love, and holiness? Will the world see Christians who have sincere hearts that long to serve the Lord? Or will they see people sarcastically rolling their eyes and refusing to obey out of childish frustration?

Proverbs 11:14 tells us, "Where there is no guidance, a people falls, but in an abundance of counselors there is safety." If we apply this to our acts of Civil Disobedience, Christians need to ensure that we are not only seeking guidance to be in accordance with the Word in our actions, but we should also be available for those who stand against injustice outside of Christ, in the ultimate hope that they will come to know God.

If those who committed violence in LA or Charlottesville had sought the guidance of true, devout Christians, their anger should have been expressed differently, as their hearts could have been transformed to know who God is and how great His love.

But as the world slides away from Judeo-Christian values and every man's "truth" is his own, there is no longer safety. Mankind becomes victims of their own selfish standards and chaos and destruction will always be the end result.

In the Garden of Gethsemane, when the Jewish guards arrested Jesus, Peter pulled out his sword and cut off the ear of Malchus. Jesus healed Malchus's ear and rebuked Peter, saying, "He who lives by the sword dies by the sword."[122]

When Peter used violence to cut off the man's ear, he in essence was doing exactly what we do when we engage in violence. We figuratively cut off the ears of all those around us, preventing them from hearing the Word of God.

Peter, after receiving the Holy Spirit, experienced a change of heart and understood his role and the role of all Christians in this World. In 1 Peter 2:9-12, Peter stated,

> "But you are not like that, for you are a chosen people. You are royal priests, a holy nation, God's very own possession. As a result, you can show others the goodness of God, for he called you out of the darkness into his wonderful light.

> "Once you had no identity as a people;
>   now you are God's people.
> Once you received no mercy;
>   now you have received God's mercy."

---

[122] Matthew 26:47-56; Mark 14:43-50; Luke 22:47-53; John 18:10-12

Dear friends, I warn you as "temporary residents and foreigners" to keep away from worldly desires that wage war against your very souls. Be careful to live properly among your unbelieving neighbors. Then even if they accuse you of doing wrong, they will see your honorable behavior, and they will give honor to God when he judges the world.

Our version of an "uprising" should always be done with love. Moreover, it needs to be nonviolent. It needs to be acted in accordance with the laws of a loving and gracious God who seeks to unite His people to Himself and to draw in the lost.

We want others to see Jesus through our actions and for them to know God as a result of the lives that we live. Without demonstrating the way we ought to live for Christ, the lost will never know Him. Our primary duty is to engage the world in this way.

CHAPTER NINE:

When Causes Become Idols

And God spoke all these words, saying,

"I am the Lord your God, who brought you out of the land of Egypt, out of the house of slavery.

"You shall have no other gods before me.

"You shall not make for yourself a carved image, or any likeness of anything that is in heaven above, or that is in the earth beneath, or that is in the water under the earth. You shall not bow down to them or serve them, for I the Lord your God am a jealous God, visiting the iniquity of the fathers on the children to the third and the fourth generation of those who hate me, but showing steadfast love to thousands of those who love me and keep my commandments."[123]

---

[123] Exodus 20:1-6

Idolatry

If one thing is clear about human nature, it is the fact that we were made to worship. Unfortunately, as we are warned throughout the Bible, we often find ourselves choosing to worship things other than God. We often come to realize that our hearts have given us over to the things of the world or to things we deem more urgent for our attention than the Lord.

It could be work, family, or that perfect house we have been wanting to buy; but too often what we find is that our idols are rooted in covetousness. We start to ask the question, "What do *they* have that *I* don't have?"

One of the things that we hear about frequently these days is the concept of privilege. When we desperately long for the privilege that another person has, our coveting leads us to making privilege an idol. And while there are certainly some people who have privileges over others—and at times that is born out of unfairness or unjust reasons—our perspective of privilege needs to remain in contentment of our own situations, just like Paul teaches us when he says,

> "Not that I am speaking of being in need, for I have learned in whatever situation I am to be content. I know how to be brought low, and I know how to abound. In any and every circumstance, I have learned the secret of facing plenty and hunger, abundance and

need. I can do all things through him who strengthens me."[124]

But when we are not content and we crave the privilege that is supposed to make our lives easier and more streamlined, we can very easily give ourselves over to desiring something we cannot obtain. The more we want it and crave it, the more willing we are to work to get it. At times, that obsession leads us straight into this craving.

So if we crave the privilege that belongs to another, we risk growing weary of doing good[125] and loving our neighbor because we believe that it is now our turn to have that prosperousness.

Likewise, when it comes to money, it is truly unfair that some people with the same skills may be in situations of making vastly different salaries. Some people have more than others. Some people have skills that earn them more, some know the right people, some people got lucky, and yet others just worked extra hard to get what they wanted. Regardless, this is an external privilege that people are given.

But, of course, there are many other idols in this world. We can see the vast importance that cultures have pinned on carved images that they consider "gods of fertility"—from Kokopelli to Isis, Hathor, Mama Ocllo, and dozens of others.

Fertility has always been cherished throughout history—although there are some debates as to whether it is still considered a blessing in western society. In the past, however, people worshiped and prayed

---

[124] Philippians 4:11-13
[125] Galatians 6:9

to these idols because they wanted children. They wanted more, or at least *some,* of what they believed these idols offered to them.

Although the world no longer agrees on the blessing children are, we can still see many examples today of how childbirth and children can be idols. People pursue quite varied means of getting pregnant and, once they have children, they often put all their energy and devotion into raising those children. If someone else has more children, or their children are honored in athletics or academics, it is another thing they may covet or desire for their own lives. And for those who struggle with fertility, bitterness can take root when they see others who get pregnant easily.

And when someone we know has more money, privilege, kids, or success than us due to reasons we cannot control, the only thing we *can* control is our response. We can choose to respond with joy for their sake. We can choose to let it motivate us for our sake. Or we can choose frustration that we do not have those same chances or anger because we want something they have.[126]

But when we are involved in an act of civil disobedience, when we are fighting for justice in the name of Christ for a cause, we risk another form of idolatry. And while we must refrain from having covetous thoughts, we also need to find the balance of standing firm in the faith and not making our cause our idol.

The Patriot's View

---

[126] Teddy Roosevelt said, "Comparison is the thief of joy." When we compare our circumstances to others, wanting what they have, we are saying, "God, You messed up by not giving me what they have."

Among all the idols in this world, politics can stand near the top.

In days like these we are in, when it seems as though politics determine the freedom of Christians to live in line with Scripture, there is a very compelling reason to fight for our politics. But as soon as we grow more passionate about the movement or cause than the truth of Christ, we have given ourselves over to idolatry.

When I speak to groups, it is common for people to come up to me to share their thoughts on the topic, ask for prayer, or offer words of encouragement. When I speak during an election season, inevitably a person will walk up with a campaign sticker or tag to talk to me about the election they are involved in.

What I am most often told is that God is in line with the Republican party and our duty is to vote out the Democrats.

This is simply untrue.

While the Republican party does share a lot of traditional Judeo-Christian views, and the Democrat party strays into progressive beliefs that do not strictly adhere to these views, that does *not* by any means tell us that the Republican party is God's party—or that they are His chosen people to declare the way of the Lord.

How do we know this?

First of all, in applying our test, we see that nowhere does Jesus or the Bible talk about our American two-party system. Our responsibility is to God and not to the political process.

Secondly, since God raises up leaders[127], our democratic process does not get to veto the leaders He raises up. I doubt God gets

---

[127] Daniel 2:21

frustrated by our elections, even though He will turn us over to these leaders based on the values we represent.[128]

Further, there are some Republican values that are not in line with Scripture. One of those values is this very ethic—the idea of putting ones' country in a place of primary importance.

Not all Republicans are believers in Christ. For instance, male-to-female transexual YouTuber Blaire White is both nonreligious and a conservative who openly voted for Donald Trump, accepting the backlash from the progressive community[129]. When Republicanism is equated with righteousness and the quest to honor God, we diminish the Creator of the universe to an institution that has existed for less than two-hundred years and includes digergent viewpoints of what is and isn't holy.

Likewise, there are many Democrats who truly believe that the social aspects of liberalism are strongly rooted in the commandment to love our neighbors as ourselves. They believe that this is a better representation of Christ-like care for others than anything offered by the Republican party and that, because this is the second greatest commandment, it supersedes other moral issues.

There is so much to be said for this point, but if we look at human nature versus the mercy of God, we can see that it is not our political party that proves our Christianity. Whatever our political affiliation may be, we have a personal responsibility to demonstrate truth and the grace of Christ to all people at all times.

---

[128] 1 Samuel 8:18, Acts 17:26, Hosea 8:4; Romans 13:1;
[129] ..Do i regret voting trump? (2018, January 20). Retrieved April 12, 2021, from https://www.youtube.com/watch?v=vNm5tz1rW0A

But a political idol doesn't have to align with a political party. Take another look at the Freeman movement. In this, the devotion to fighting against unjust tax laws is so strong that followers of this ideology place it above what we were told in Scripture and refuse to "render unto Caesar."

This is down to the interpretation of the law, which is not as easy as it sounds. In truth, the use of our taxes may violate our consciences, but it also violated the consciences of those who questioned Jesus about this issue, and He made no provisions for allowing people to skip tax day because of how the government would unjustly use those taxes.

Justice for Jesus

There are some incredibly important issues of social justice that Christians must take a stand on. It is deeply important that we are doers of the Word[130] and that we demonstrate our faith through works, even if that is not the root of our salvation.

Still, we need clear reasons for our actions while preventing those actions from becoming idols in our lives. Acting on justice is important and even admirable for Christians, but does that mean that it should be our primary aim in life? Not at all. Our primary aim is to glorify God and enjoy him forever.[131]

In practice, what does it look like to idolize our need to be the hands and feet of Christ?

---

[130] James 1:22-27
[131] The Westminster Catechism Question #1

All true followers of Jesus can agree that sex-trafficking is a vile, twisted, abomination of a sin. It is the opposite of loving our neighbor. It devalues humanity and degrades a holy act that God created between husband and wife into a violent transaction. It is the duty of Christians and the Church to fight against this sin.

There are even governments where sex-trafficking is either unregulated or it is covered up for the sake of lucrative sex-tourist dollars that boost the local economy.[132] When the government openly or secretly defends and protects such heinous human rights violations, Christians must stand up and fight instead.

But what is our reason for fighting? Is it to see to it that every child is free? Are we fighting to ensure that young women are not kept, abused, and left suffering upon having unsupported children of their own?

These are noble goals, but we are called to something higher.

These righteous and worthwhile acts shouldn't be worshiped. Nor should our pride in being a part of the fight become an idol. Instead of worshiping the fight against human trafficking, our fight

---

[132] This includes countries such as Thailand and the Netherlands where sex tourism is legal and sex-trafficking and sexual exploitation directly result from lax policies. However, there have been other countries where there are defined laws against human trafficking that have been accused of not enforcing policies for the sake of economics. A few countries which have faced these accusations have been Brazil, Mexico, Cambodia, and the Philippines.

Ward-Pelar, J. (2010, April 01). Rationalizing sexual tourism: How some countries benefit from selling sex. Retrieved April 12, 2021, from http://www.inquiriesjournal.com/articles/235/rationalizing-sexual-tourism-how-some-countries-benefit-from-selling-sex

Cambodia - United States Department of state. (2020, December 01). Retrieved April 12, 2021, from https://www.state.gov/reports/2020-trafficking-in-persons-report/cambodia/

must first be an *act of* worship to the Lord. <u>Love for the Lord comes first. Love for people comes second.</u>

While there is absolutely nothing wrong with fighting against sex-trafficking from a moral perspective—and non-Christians do this frequently—for those who have given their lives to Christ, this fight must have a higher goal. Otherwise, we risk worshiping ourselves or the women and children we protect, and we risk growing prideful because of our efforts. We also risk falling into hopelessness and despair when we see just how vile sin has caused the world to be. And when Christians get lost in the cause instead of the purpose, *we* are ultimately the ones who are glorified.

While the fight against sex-trafficking is a pretty major issue, we can see it in many social justice movements. We see it in the fight against poverty through fair trade and ethical businesses, which can become an idol for those who make conscious choices to purchase brands that have a greater social purpose. We see it in child sponsorship programs that work to break the cycle of poverty. In truth, we see it in so many moral arenas that it is deeply important to always ask ourselves if we are worshiping a cause or if we are worshiping the Creator of truth and justice.

Where Does the Church Stand?

It is not only individual Christians who need to recognize our bias toward idolatry. Churches must do the same.

For instance, many people claim that if all churchgoers would stop engaging in the use of pornography, the-porn industry would virtually go bankrupt. In one survey, over 50% of pastors and 68% of men who regularly attend church admitted to viewing pornography on a regular basis.[133]

This is not a new problem. During the pre-Capone gang times, Christians responded to alcohol and prostitution in Chicago. A protest was led into the levee—Chicago's red-light district—and the prostitutes said that after the protests, the area had never been livelier as so many young evangelists decided to stay to try out the darker side of life.[134]

When we consider that anywhere between 50-80% of trafficked victims are filmed for pornographic purposes, we can also acknowledge the very real and awful problem of the fact that a significant amount of porn depicts true violence and assault against those in the videos—most often the women[135].

Pornography is an idol for many. It eats away at their souls as an addiction and leads people away from God and away from their families. Recent studies have shown that a tenth of 12- to 13-year-

---

[133] User, S. (n.d.). Publications the entry of his Word restoring the Years: Winning the battle over sexual addiction and PORNOGRAPHY restoring the years: A Healing workbook for Women dealing with their Husband's Pornography / sexual ADDICTION restoring the YEARS [WORKBOOK REVIEW]. Retrieved April 12, 2021, from https://ankyrapublications.com/help-trafficked-victims

November 01, 2. (n.d.). 15 mind-blowing statistics about pornography and the church. Retrieved April 12, 2021, from https://www.missionfrontiers.org/issue/article/15-mind-blowing-statistics-about-pornography-and-the-church

[134] Kobler, John "Capone: The Life and World of Al Capone Da Capo press 2003 p34-37

[135] Dimitri B September 26th, Jenna Funk July 15th, Kelly Rippa December 25th, Jenny Yasi December 26th, R Hart January 10th, Sky November 16th, . . . *, N. (2020, July 08). How pornography impacts violence against women and child sex abuse. Retrieved April 12, 2021, from https://www.focusforhealth.org/how-pornography-impacts-violence-against-women-and-child-sex-abuse/

olds fear they are already addicted to pornography.[136] The Church has to actively work to fight against it.

In that fight, the Church has to keep the focus on Christ. Purity is a wonderful thing, but we can't allow the idol of pornography to be replaced by the idol of purity. It is truly only Jesus who can heal this addiction in a healthy way.

There are ample resources for overcoming a porn addiction, and for the 68% of Christian men who view porn on a regular basis and the 87% of Christian women who have, at some point, watched porn in their lives, these resources need to be utilized.

Perhaps one of the most important resources we have available to us is our pastors. Pastors who do not engage in the use of pornography, and who are prepared to work with those in the congregation who struggle in this area, are an excellent source of wisdom and guidance.

However, one other thing to note is the evangelical obsession with purity and how this "salvation through abstinence" mentality can actually contribute to sexual sin in a number of ways.

One of the ways the idol of purity contributes to porn use is the false belief that it isn't "real sex," so it doesn't count as sexual sin.

First of all, not only have we already looked at the fact that people *do* get hurt in the making of pornography through assault and sex-slavery, but porn also significantly rewires our brains and can cause unhealthy sexuality between us and our future spouse. Moreover, the Bible is very clear when Jesus said,

---

[136] Howse, Patrick "Pornography addiction worry" for tenth of 12- to 13-year-olds BBC.com 31 March 2015

"But I say to you that everyone who looks at a woman with lustful intent has already committed adultery with her in his heart. If your right eye causes you to sin, tear it out and throw it away. For it is better that you lose one of your members than that your whole body be thrown into hell. And if your right hand causes you to sin, cut it off and throw it away. For it is better that you lose one of your members than that your whole body go into hell."

The idol of purity can also distract from a healthy view of sex within marriage by creating shame—something it shares with the idol of pornography.

Shame ultimately separates us from God, and that is the greatest concern when it comes to idols. If we allow our hearts to be polluted by worshiping something other than God, whether that idol is a sinful act or an act of morality, it pulls us from the ultimate goal of glorifying God.

As a final note on how this applies to the Church as a whole is the preoccupation many churches have with acts of social care.

Again, this is engaging in being the hands and feet of Jesus. This is a good thing! But when churches are shallow in the Gospel but rich in works, they are still missing the primary aim.

As an example, there is a church in Florida that does amazing work in the community. They do a significant amount of outreach to the homeless and give care and support to the downtrodden. They offer help with food, rent, clothing, reintegration after prison life, foster care, and many other wonderful things.

This church is known in the community for being good and gracious people. They do not restrict their services to those who are believers in Jesus and will give the coat on their back to whomever needs it.

And when people come to a church service for the first time?

Unfortunately, this church has an aversion to using more than one Bible verse per sermon and, at times, there are none used at all. During Communion one Sunday, the pastor suggested that if people didn't want to get up to get the Communion cups in the back, they could just drink the coffee and eat the donut they had gotten during the greeting time (these are provided by the church each Sunday). The claim was that the elements don't matter, only the heart behind it matters.

But this isn't necessarily true. The elements in Communion are set apart to be *holy*. Our breakfast is our breakfast. Our set apart moment of coming to the table to meet with Jesus is where we meet His holiness.

So when a church does wonderful work to be the hands and feet of Jesus but struggles on very basic theological principles while avoiding the use of Scripture in sermons, it is difficult to deny that the mission of the church has been placed above the importance of salvation, justification, and sanctification.

Through these significantly varied examples, the biggest thing we can see is the responsibility of the Church in guiding people to know Christ and to truly give their lives over to Him as their one and only God, above all else.

Idolatry in Cults and False Prophets

False prophets generally engage in their antics for one of two reasons:

1. They are frauds.
2. They are crazy.

Whichever the problem, these false prophets seek to delude people into following them. They desire the power and control that come with their position, and they seek to become a deity of their own making.

It is not uncommon for these cult leaders to pop up now and then, and it is not uncommon for us to hear tragic stories of how these leaders bring an end to their reign.

When we look at someone like David Koresh of the Waco siege, it really is hard to tell if he truly believed that he was an instrument of God or if he was a power-hungry narcissist. Either way, he allowed his worship of self to lead him down a path of destruction. Ultimately, among his Branch Davidian followers, there were 79 deaths as a result of his beliefs. Koresh himself was shot in the head and killed.[137]

---

[137] Murray, James "Followers of cult leader David Koresh still under his spell 25 years after Waco inferno" Express 25 February 2018

But when insanity or narcissism lead us deeper into the natural, human desire to be the god of our own lives, we can see that this is not all that uncommon. It may not always look as extreme as Koresh in Waco, but all things can be taken too far.

Whether our idols are admirable things like justice issues or horrific things like cult leadership, we still need to take the time to redirect our focus and turn our eyes upon Jesus, the Author and Finisher of our faith.

Subject to Governmental Authorities

In discussing idols and idolatry, we have looked at a number of different issues. But as it relates to our Civil Disobedience, we can see that many of these things are cultural norms that are worshiped around us, and we must fight to not give in to them.

However, one of these issues is still that of governance. What do we do when we want to fight against the government for the sake of our idols as opposed to the sake of the Gospel? What do we do when our political affiliation appears more morally Christian than the ruling party and we dislike how they are leading us?

We can turn to Paul's words in Romans 13:2, which say, "Therefore whoever resists the authorities resists what God has appointed, and those who resist will incur judgment."

We know that we are not meant to obey the government when they actually incite us to sin. For instance, those governments who allow for sex trafficking cannot force a Christian to *engage* in that because we know that it is against the truth, and we would never subject ourselves to that sort of authority.

But when we are angry about a party who is in leadership and we see that they are making decisions that go against Christianity, we must bear in mind Paul's words. We were never promised that we would love our government, its rulers, or their laws and decisions. But we are instructed to honor that the Lord appointed them.

God is sovereign. We cannot change that. The party leaders cannot change that. We can only accept that He has put them in a position of leading the country for a reason, and we can trust that He will accomplish His purposes.

The moment we question God's decision to appoint certain leaders, we are making an idol of ourselves by believing that we know better than God. We are resisting His appointing, and we will incur judgment as a result.

If it seems like a convoluted thing to obey our leaders unless they ask us to sin, it's not. All we can do is turn to the Word of the Lord, meditating on Scripture and seeking God in prayer. He will guide us, and He will ultimately reign over all.

CHAPTER TEN:

Consequences of Civil Disobedience

"Blessed are those who are persecuted for righteousness' sake, for theirs is the kingdom of heaven.

"Blessed are you when others revile you and persecute you and utter all kinds of evil against you falsely on my account. Rejoice and be glad, for your reward is great in heaven, for so they persecuted the prophets who were before you."

-Matthew 5:10-12

THE "BEATITUDES" ARE A PASSAGE THAT REMIND US OF THE blessings that come from having right "attitudes." They are a list of characteristics that the Lord considers to be worthy of blessing and favor.

We love to think of His promises of blessings as physical rewards, especially when we are the recipients! But we do not like some of His other promises that say we are blessed when we suffer for His sake.

Many of us who have realized this blessing can easily romanticize the idea of the Lord's favor when we have suffered for His sake. It is less easy to romanticize the actual suffering.

Sure, we can think about it in terms of a Renaissance painting of our hands clasped together in prayer as we stare out the window of our small jail cell, a dove gracefully flying by with an olive branch in its beak as a sign of peace and promise.

Or we can more accurately look through the history books and read about the pure evils of humanity and how horrifically people have been treated by others who have given into their sinful natures. And if we acknowledge the reality of this—the true depths of what it could mean to be persecuted—we also have to accept that it's not always going to be a simple portrait of hope in the midst of isolation.

Either way, what we have to accept is the fact that Christian Civil Disobedience is likely to lead to persecution. And persecution is not going to be fun.

One of the biggest issues I have seen in many of the recent protests (by all groups in the 21st century) is the sense of entitlement, thinking that they can protest without any consequences. However, to engage in any form of Civil Disobedience means there will be consequences to you. You and your ideas are not entitled to enjoy a peaceful reception from the world or from those who disagree with you.

However, if God requires you to do this, then the worldly consequences should be irrelevant. God will honor you in this world or the next, according to His purpose. As people who seek to serve Him, this should be enough for us and should be a fine motivator. Still, because we have to recognize that our purpose is to glorify God, sometimes this means that we have to suffer for His glory.

Failure to accept or recognize this means you are not engaging in Civil Disobedience as a Christian. Entitled complaints are not the same as actively working toward honoring Christ and refusing to bow to unjust or immoral belief systems under which we are placed.

Unfortunately, as history shows us, there have been many Christians who did not believe in accepting the consequences of Civil Disobedience. Sometimes, in fact, they have even been on the side of the persecutors.

Letter from a Birmingham Jail

When Martin Luther King, Jr., was in jail in Birmingham, he wrote his famous letter that is today studied by students and civil rights activists all over the United Sates and many parts of the world. He expressed frustrations with the moderate white groups, but there is not an expectation that everyone should be on his side. He did not have the entitlement factor that felt his beliefs, because they were superior or simply because they were *his*, would be wholeheartedly accepted by others.[138]

---

[138] King, Martin Luther. "Letter from Birmingham Jail." *Letter from Birmingham Jail, by Dr. Martin Luther King, Jr.*, letterfromjail.com/.

In an interview with King, he argued that those who were racists were not willing to go to jail for their cause, but those who were engaging in Civil Disobedience were willing to do so.[139] This distinction, according to King, was the reason why he knew that Civil Rights were going to win. It was not a matter of the ideology being right; it was a matter of who truly held their belief to the ultimate end.

Being able to suffer the consequences of your actions is the critical component to winning the hearts and changing the laws of a nation. There is an element of example to it, whereby others will see that you have something worth fighting for. But beyond that, it's the tenacity that we will not be willing to back down, no matter the cost.

Christ Himself says we must take up our cross[140]. In other words, we have to suffer for the sake of Jesus. He didn't offer any caveats for taking up our crosses "if it's convenient" or taking them up "until they get too heavy." The call is to follow Him.

In 2 Timothy 3:12-13, we read "Indeed, all who desire to live a godly life in Christ Jesus will be persecuted, while evil people and impostors will go on from bad to worse, deceiving and being deceived."

When the Bible says that everyone will be persecuted, I feel pretty safe to say that everyone will be persecuted. And if this applied to the Christians in the New Testament, it will apply to us as well. Knowing this, we know that consequences will come. If you find yourself as a

---

[139] NBCNews, director. *Martin Luther King, Jr. On NBC's Meet the Press (1965) | Archives | NBC News. YouTube*, NBC, 1965, www.youtube.com/watch?v=fAtsAwGreyE.
[140] Matthew 16:24

Christian adhering to views that exempt you from the persecution of the world, you must consider whether you are living "a godly life in Christ Jesus."

And, if this isn't enough, there is another unfortunate point to make. If you are engaging in Christian Civil Disobedience, do not be surprised if these worldly consequences come from within the church.

In the progressive church, we find more and more often there are those who consider orthodox Christianity to be hateful. It is popular nowadays to say that even believing in the Jesus (who claimed to be the only way to God[141]) requires loving others enough to "recognize" that all paths can lead to God.

I remember talking with a chaplain at a hospital. I was asking her about how she shared the Gospel with people who are sick or dying. I hoped to learn something from her. She responded that she doesn't share the Gospel because she was afraid she might offend someone. When I dug deeper, her response was, "I don't think God limits how people get to heaven to only Christ." I guess His crucifixion meant nothing to her.

Regardless, this is a person who is talking with people at the end of life and comforting those who are hurting. And she is doing this as a "Christian."

To disagree with her and others like her has become controversial.

---

[141] John 14:6

Many churches and cultural Christians will go on the attack, saying that you need to "love all" and give in to the unjust laws that inhibit our abilities as Christians to live according to the biblical nature of our faith.

I am not denying the right to emphasize love, but not at the expense of obedience to the Lord. "Love" that does not result in obedience is neither scriptural nor real. We see this in John 14:15, which says, "If you love me, you will keep my commandments." Ultimately, to love God and to love our neighbor requires us to be a proponent of the truth—to love them enough to demand holy justice.

During Nazi Germany, there was a split between the Confessing Church and the German Christian Church. The Confessing Church had concerns about what was happening to the Jews and maintained the slogan, "The church must remain church."[142] It was attacked frequently by the German Christian Church, which was more nationalist, attacking all things that were not Aryan. So many Christians—like Dietrich Bonhoeffer who stood up to the Nazis through acts of Civil Disobedience—were opposed by the German Christian movement, which subsequently labeled all opponents as Jewish.[143] The purpose was to immobilize the Confessing Church and those who used their faith to stand up to the tyranny that was around them.

---

[142] Bergen, p12
[143] Bergen, p32-33

Oddly enough, we are seeing the same *vast generalization* strategy at work today, attempting to turn others against the Christians who defy cultural norms. Christians are considered "sexist" or "patriarchal" because the Bible values life in the womb[144] and because of complementarian views sometimes cited in Genesis 2:18, Ephesians 5:21-33, and Titus 2:3-5. The list goes on. There are so many topics which could be covered, but it always comes down to one-word labels meant to make us look bad and leave a bad impression of us as being the enemy.

I don't expect people outside the Church to understand our views. I do expect them to ridicule us just as I did when I was living outside of God's Word. But the discouraging part is how often these ideas are being touted even within the Church at large.

Who Will Stand?

A deeply important thing to note in light of all of this is that Martin Luther King's famous letter was written to Christian pastors in the church.[145] To stand up for God (in spite of public pressure to engage in the world system) means mainstream churches may not support us. And it will often be the case that we are made an example of to make the prominent "Christian message" appear more palatable to the world.

---

[144] Psalm 139, Isaiah 44:24
[145] King, Martin Luther. "Letter from Birmingham Jail." *Letter from Birmingham Jail, by Dr. Martin Luther King, Jr.*, letterfromjail.com/.

Sadly, too many Christian churches prioritize increased attendance and monetizing their ministries, so they avoid being controversial and give in to public pressure.

During the end of times, we know that we will see large amounts of ungodliness, but we also know that we will see where the church will express a form of godliness while denying its power.

> But understand this, that in the last days there will come times of difficulty. For people will be lovers of self, lovers of money, proud, arrogant, abusive, disobedient to their parents, ungrateful, unholy, heartless, unappeasable, slanderous, without self-control, brutal, not loving good, treacherous, reckless, swollen with conceit, lovers of pleasure rather than lovers of God, having the appearance of godliness, but denying its power. Avoid such people.[146]

It is shocking to see how familiar that is to many of the messages touted by popular churches. The lovers of self are constantly searching how to live their best lives now; meanwhile the abusive hide in plain sight as highly praised pastors and apologists. Children may reject their parents in order to find support from church leaders to "be their true selves" while the parents are denied rights[147] to raise

---

[146] 2 Timothy 3:1-5
[147] Kao, E. (n.d.). Pelosi's equality act could lead to more parents losing custody of kids who want "GENDER Transition". Retrieved April 12, 2021, from https://www.heritage.org/marriage-and-family/commentary/pelosis-equality-act-could-lead-more-parents-losing-custody-kids-who

their children within biblical Christianity. And while persecution of any kind can be brutal, persecution that leads to a beloved child being taken away is torturous.

But this is the world we are living in, just as the writers of the Bible predicted. These people are to be avoided, even though they have the appearance of godliness. It is because of this that we cannot trust the flesh but must test everything through the lens of Bible, God's Word—the only objective standard of Truth.

And if we do find these characteristics in our own hearts and are having to test ourselves against the Bible? We should most certainly listen to the wisdom of Thomas Guthrie, who warned of these days when he said, "Anticipate the day when you shall behold a God in judgment and a world in flames. Flee to Jesus now. Escape from the wrath to come. To come? In a sense wrath has already come. The fire has caught, it—has seized your garments; delay, and you are wrapt in flames. Oh! haste away, and throw yourselves into the fountain which has, power to quench these fires, and cleanse you from all your sins."[148]

Ireland to India

When Amy Carmichael decided to become a missionary shortly before the turn of the twentieth century, she did not know what her mission would look like. She did not know that her poor health would lead her to India. She did not know that she would end up on

---

[148] "The Gospel in Ezekiel" Thomas Guthrie, 1857.

mission to rescue young girls from temple prostitution. But that was exactly where God led her.

The religious leaders at the time were not always fans of Carmichael. She was known for having a bold and even difficult personality[149] and she wasn't afraid to point out when there was a lack of Scriptural use in the church. In fact, although some of her own interpretations of the Bible were questioned, she was unwilling to waver on the importance of Scripture in her work.

Amy rescued children from the brothels of India against the will of the religious leaders. Some thought she made too big a deal about it or that it was a political stunt. And there were those who thought it was not worth the effort to change hundreds of years of history and culture.

When we look at some of her tactics, Amy would be decried in modern times for her "appropriation" of Indian clothing—which she wore as a sign of respect—and for the fact that she would stain her skin with coffee so she could go unnoticed as she sought to rescue these young girls.

Amy was bold, and she was not afraid to challenge the culture she was in. She was not intimidated by the many Christian leaders who had been in India before her and had made no effort to handle this issue. In seeing their unwillingness to make a change, she chose to do it herself.

---

[149] Murray, I. (2015, April 01). Amy Carmichael. Retrieved April 12, 2021, from https://www.thegospelcoalition.org/reviews/amy-carmichael/

Of course, this is aside from the persecution she faced from the temple leaders from whom she actually rescued these children, and those in the community who would pressure her to give the children back for the sake of sexual abuse.

The truth we see through Amy's life is the tragedy that a lot of people will remain silent. They will remain silent to "respect" culture when it is really just cowardice. They will remain silent to show "love" when it is really just fear of being called out.

Many in the church remain silent about abortion. Many remain silent about pornography, despite the fact that it is destroying lives and the dignity of our bodies. And many will remain silent about marriage—whether it is destroyed by things such as pornography, affairs, or even the lack of effort to pursue the interlocking pieces of love and respect.

Therefore, even if you have a legitimate Biblical foundation, do not expect the Church to speak on your behalf. They might not care about you and the issue you are willing to stand up for. And when the world follows the flesh and pollutes the church, we must live with the hope that we will have support from true Christ-followers, even though we are not entitled to that support.

I would even go so far as to say there should be an expectation to go to jail. After all, to stand up against an unjust law does not deny the fact that the unjust law is still the law of the land with consequences for violating it.

In fact, Gandhi held that the goal of Civil Disobedience was to go to prison. Accomplishing this was to show people how much you care, and this was considered the start to changing people's hearts.[150] He did not act out of a love for Christian truths, but he believed enough in his mission to aim for his personal goal of prison.

This goal to go to prison as a Christian will send a similar message to nonbelievers everywhere. They will watch with curiosity and start to question why you would be willing to suffer. Once they start asking these questions, their hearts start to open for the Holy Spirit to move and make a difference.

Nelson Mandela, for instance, was in prison for twenty-seven years because of his determination to follow the pragmatic aspect of Gandhi's demonstrations. As he fought against apartheid, he was willing to spend more than a quarter of a century in prison in the hopes that hearts would be changed.[151]

And we must decide whether or not we are willing to do the same thing. The world will do what it needs to do to stop us. So, before you engage in the act of Civil Disobedience, you must know that there is a possibility that your obedience to God will not only lead to suffering but could also lead to death.

There are many historical examples of those who engaged in Civil Disobedience and died for their cause. Gandhi and Martin Luther King Jr. both were assassinated. Gandhi faced his assassination by gunpoint for being too accommodating to other religions. Martin Luther King Jr. survived a knife attack and was, ultimately, assassinated by gunpoint as well. Dietrich Bonhoeffer was executed

---

[150] Shephard Mark "Mahatma Gandhi and His Myths, Simple Productions 2011 p 31
[151] Nelson Mandela's prison numbers. (n.d.). Retrieved April 12, 2021, from https://www.nelsonmandela.org/content/page/prison-timeline

by hanging at the Flossenbürg concentration camp, a mere two weeks before the camp was liberated by the U.S. military.

However, these men are not the only ones who died as a result of Civil Disobedience they believed in. And Bonhoeffer is certainly not the only man who died for the cause of Christ. There are countless ancient and modern Christians who have died for the Gospel.[152]

Secular Civil Disobedience can inspire us, and martyrdom can be a consequence; but Christian Civil Disobedience is about taking up our cross to follow Christ. The suffering that will result—even to the extent of martyrdom—is not about human rights. It is about a heart that is wholly devoted to the worship of God, even if it means we have to die.

However, all is not lost. You have every reason to be proud of any suffering you have experienced. People of this world will try to shame you, but we receive our Truth straight from the Word of God.

Hebrews 10:32-39 says,

> Remember those earlier days after you had received the light, when you endured in a great conflict full of suffering. Sometimes you were publicly exposed to insult and persecution; at other times you stood side by side with those who were so treated. You suffered along with those in prison and joyfully accepted the

---

[152] 12, D., Daniel Philpott is associate professor of political science and peace studies at the University of Notre Dame., Cindy Wooden - Catholic News ServiceApril 12, Yonat Shimron - Religion News ServiceApril 12, Matt Sedensky - Associated PressApril 12, & 11, D. (2014, August 15). Modern Martyrs: Thousands die for their faith each year. How should the CHURCH RESPOND? Retrieved April 12, 2021, from https://www.americamagazine.org/issue/modern-martyrs

confiscation of your property, because you knew that you yourselves had better and lasting possessions. So do not throw away your confidence; it will be richly rewarded.

You need to persevere so that when you have done the will of God, you will receive what he has promised. For,

"In just a little while,

he who is coming will come

and will not delay."

And,

"But my righteous one will live by faith.

And I take no pleasure

in the one who shrinks back."

But we do not belong to those who shrink back and are destroyed, but to those who have faith and are saved.

(emphasis added)

This passage, written to Christians in Rome, was written during times of immense persecution. The Roman Emperor Nero, was considered one of the most ruthless rulers of the empire. Yet the writer of Hebrews reminded them that they were persecuted early on through ridicule, prison, and the confiscation of property; but they could tolerate this because real Christian possessions are lasting. They wanted to give up, but we are reminded that as long as we remain righteous that we will be saved and that if we shrink back, it will anger Jesus.

For instance, we are told in 1 Peter 4:16 "However, if you suffer as a Christian, do not be ashamed, but praise God that you bear that name."

Likewise, in 2 Timothy 2:12 "If we suffer, we shall also reign with him: if we deny him, he also will deny us:"

Indeed, blessed are the those who are persecuted for righteousness' sake, for theirs is the kingdom of heaven. This is a gift to us. It may not look like a gift. It will be painful. It will crush us at times.

But, as we carry our cross, He is worth the splinters we will bear.

CHAPTER ELEVEN:

Praying for Our Leaders

"Let every person be subject to the governing authorities. For there is no authority except from God, and those that exist have been instituted by God. Therefore whoever resists the authorities resists what God has appointed, and those who resist will incur judgment. For rulers are not a terror to good conduct, but to bad. Would you have no fear of the one who is in authority? Then do what is good, and you will receive his approval, for he is God's servant for your good. But if you do wrong, be afraid, for he does not bear the sword in vain. For he is the servant of God, an avenger who carries out God's wrath on the wrongdoer. Therefore one must be in subjection, not only to avoid God's wrath but also for the sake of conscience. For because of this you also pay taxes, for the authorities are ministers of God, attending to this very thing. Pay to all what is owed to them: taxes to

whom taxes are owed, revenue to whom revenue is owed, respect to whom respect is owed, honor to whom honor is owed."

Romans 13:1-7

IN A NATION DIVIDED, THERE IS LITTLE SURPRISING ABOUT THE FACT that we struggle to respect the authorities on the "other" side. From chimes of *not my President* to mockery about their clumsiness or poor choice of words—it's easy to make the leaders of "the other side" into targets for teasing.

Although this can be tempting and even understandable when we think the other side is behaving in an immoral and abhorrent way, we have to test our desires against Scripture and what we are told in the Bible.

Whether we like it or not, we have been given guidance in how to behave toward our leaders, even when we do not wish to listen to them or to show them any genuine respect.

When we read these words, it is easy for Christians to contend that the arguments of Scripture could not *possibly* apply to the leaders we are facing today. "These leaders are terrors to good conduct. Plain and simple. They are not servants of God! That would require genuine morality."

To reconcile this fact with what we read in the Bible, we have no choice but to look at the leader Paul was writing under in his letter to the Romans.

The Criminal Emperor

Nero Claudius Caesar Augustus Germanicus was the fifth emperor of Rome. In his time as emperor, he had his mother, possibly his stepbrother, his wife, and possibly his second wife murdered[153], which is nothing to say of how he treated other people.

Nero's mother, Agrippina, gives us some insight into his behavior in a sort of Norman Bates-esque manner. Overly controlling, cruel—and possibly the murderer of Nero's adoptive father, Emperor Claudius (her second husband and uncle) and his first wife—it is said that she made every effort to lead his life and his decisions.

So, he had her killed.

In Baiae, Nero spent time feasting. His feasts, however, were not only about food but excitement with music and art, as well as sex and debauchery. He is famous for *allegedly* having started a mass fire in Rome to expand his palace and rebuild the city center[154] and playing his fiddle while Rome burned.

According to the ancient writer, Tacitus,

> Nero fastened the guilt and inflicted the most exquisite tortures on a class hated for their abominations, called Christians by the populace. Mockery of every sort was added to their deaths. Covered with the skins of beasts, they were torn by dogs

[153] The Nero Files ~ Seven Things You May Not Know about Nero [Video file]. (2021, March 23). Retrieved April 12, 2021, from https://www.pbs.org/wnet/secrets/seven-things-may-not-know-nero/3416/

[154] Jarus, O. (2013, October 08). Emperor Nero: Facts & BIOGRAPHY. Retrieved April 12, 2021, from https://www.livescience.com/40277-emperor-nero-facts.html

and perished, or were nailed to crosses, or were doomed to the flames and burnt, to serve as nightly illumination when daylight had expired.[155]

Ultimately, Nero's behavior was so abominable that he was rejected by everyone, even his own guard, and led to his suicide at age thirty.[156]

Nero is known as one of the greatest enemies of early Christianity (and was thusly used by God to drastically spread the message of the Gospel as a result of this persecution). He was considered to be something of an antichrist as a result.

This is the leader under which Paul wrote Romans 13. This is the man he considered to be appointed by God. What does this tell us?

There are no precluding circumstances in respecting authorities and praying for our leaders.

Those Christians who were tortured and persecuted under Nero were unlikely to have given in to his ways or deny the truth they lived for, but their Civil Disobedience would not have been obedient to the Lord if they had been disrespectful or even violent against him.

Paul is very clear in this passage about the fact that God has given leaders their authority, and it is important that we acknowledge that as well and give the best of ourselves as citizens, even under what we perceive to be corruption. The greatest peace we can find is

---

[155] Tacitus on the Christians. (n.d.). Retrieved April 12, 2021, from
https://www.livius.org/sources/content/tacitus/tacitus-on-the-christians/
[156] The approaching end. (n.d.). Retrieved April 12, 2021, from
https://www.britannica.com/biography/Nero-Roman-emperor/The-approaching-end

the knowledge that God is sovereign, and whomever He designates for leadership has been designated for a reason.

Just as Christianity thrived under the persecution of Nero, spreading far and wide, so it can today as we see society drift further away from Christian ideals.

Every Good Work

Similar to the passage in Romans, Titus 3 gives us insight into the need for submission.

> Remind them to be submissive to rulers and authorities, to be obedient, to be ready for every good work, to speak evil of no one, to avoid quarreling, to be gentle, and to show perfect courtesy toward all people. For we ourselves were once foolish, disobedient, led astray, slaves to various passions and pleasures, passing our days in malice and envy, hated by others and hating one another. But when the goodness and loving kindness of God our Savior appeared, he saved us, not because of works done by us in righteousness, but according to his own mercy, by the washing of regeneration and renewal of the Holy Spirit, whom he poured out on us richly through Jesus Christ our Savior, so that being justified by his grace we might become heirs according to the hope of eternal life.

What we see here is that we are not just meant to obey rulers for the sake of naive obedience. We are meant to submit because (a) we are meant to be examples to others of 'perfect courtesy' and (b) we, too, were saved by the love of God, the regeneration of the Holy Spirit, and the justification of Christ.

And as we are shown through 2 Peter 1:13-17,

> Be subject for the Lord's sake to every human institution, whether it be to the emperor as supreme, or to governors as sent by him to punish those who do evil and to praise those who do good. For this is the will of God, that by doing good you should put to silence the ignorance of foolish people. Live as people who are free, not using your freedom as a cover-up for evil, but living as servants of God. Honor everyone. Love the brotherhood. Fear God. Honor the emperor.

Scripture is consistent about these two things. We are meant to live in obedience to Christ in all things, no matter the cost. We are also meant to be obedient to our ruling authorities. When these two things contradict one another, we live in the tension of Civil Disobedience. We find ourselves in the space of honoring God first and respectfully turning away from cooperation with sin. Although our leaders may not view our actions as respectful, we understand that we are to avoid quarreling and show perfect courtesy.

In these times, when we watch our leaders give themselves over to corruption, lies, and injustice, we have no choice other than to pray for them. If they are truly persecuting us, we are told in Matthew 5:44 that we are to pray for them. And what should these prayers look like?

They should not be prayers of demise, because only God is in control of who lives and who dies. They should not be prayers of despondency, because we can still have hope in the Lord through all things. Ultimately, we can pray, in faith, that the Lord will turn their hearts—that these leaders will know Him and come to salvation. We can pray that He will remove them from their positions if they do not, but we must always be subject to God's sovereignty and not begrudge the fact that He may *want* these leaders in their roles.

As we struggle to pray for those leaders who persecute us, and as we eagerly pray for the safety and protection of Christian leaders and pastors who may face persecution before we do as a result of their office, we should also pray for our own hearts to be softened toward our enemies and to be bold with the truth.

Putting on the Armor

Whether engaging in Civil Disobedience or responding to the persecution that comes from it, the Bible gives us a clear example of what it looks like to stand firm in the ways God leads us.

Paul was a great example of one who handled both Civil Disobedience and persecution. Whether he was preaching the Gospel against the law or whether he was suffering persecution, Paul stayed true to his purpose of sharing the Gospel.

His steadfastness caused him to be beaten multiple times and landed him in prison multiple times, and ultimately he was beheaded for speaking the Truth. This former Jewish leader who persecuted Christians was a prime example of the mercy of God, as Paul wrote in the verses we looked at from Titus 3.

While he was in Jerusalem, Paul spoke to a crowd about Jesus, and a mob formed. It was so bad that Roman soldiers had to carry him above their heads to help him get through the mob. Paul convinced them to let him down so he could speak to the mob, and he started telling them about Jesus again.

During the first time he was in prison in Rome, he was able to illustrate how Christians ought to act when facing persecution. At this point in time he had already faced prison in Philippi, been chased out of Thessalonica, scrutinized in Athens, persecuted in Corinth, and chased out of Jerusalem. He was no stranger to persecution on either side. He had once been the one actively pursuing punishment for those who believed in Jesus, and he was now one of the pursued.

There is a spiritual component to engaging in Civil Disobedience as a Christian. Whatever the cause we engage in, it must be something that has stirred in our spirit. For example, as soon as I obey God or refuse to follow an evil law based on His Truth as an act of Civil Disobedience, my act becomes spiritual in nature. Furthermore, when we are persecuted for it by those who are against God, we know that their response is a spiritual action.

Many Christians assume that spiritual attacks are "dramatic" and "Hollywood" in essence. Yet spiritual attacks can't always be visually seen or manifested in the people who are persecuting us, even though the spiritual realm is still the ultimate source. What comes out of their mouths is what is in their hearts and in their souls. That's why Paul made it very clear when he said that our battle is not against flesh and blood.

He would not have said that if it were not spiritual, manifested in flesh and blood or others.

Whether he was inspired by the Roman soldiers that kept guard of him in prison or weather he was just so used to the volume of the soldiers present in that region, Paul was able to use the illustration of the Roman armor to describe how to respond to a spiritual attack.

Paul's response was simple. He told us that we need to put on the armor of God.

Ephesians 6:13 tells us, "Therefore take up the whole armor of God, that you may be able to withstand in the evil day, and having done all, to stand firm." This passage then goes on to explain what that looks like and what it means for us in our daily lives.

This is a common "Christianese" response. "Put on the armor of God, and you will be okay." But I have found that many Christians walking through trials do not always understand how to put on this seemingly imaginary armor. If I put on an armor that I do not see, am I not the new subject of "the Emperor's new clothes?"

There are many books written about the armor of God. I have read many of them, and my notes about the armor of God get placed in the front of every journal and added to as I learn more. I say this as there are many Christian influences on this topic, but I do not know which one taught me what point. Therefore, I apologize for the lack of citations on these topics. I am by no way trying to pass this off as my own, but I think those who are preparing to stand up for God's Truth need this information.[157]

Belt of Truth: This is God's Truth

Paul starts the armor here because, as with Roman soldiers, without the belt, the rest of the armor will fall off. The belt holds the rest of the armor together. Since the belt is God's Truth, without God's truth, you have **no** answer.

Whether you are looking at when to engage in Civil Disobedience or when there is persecution in response, God's Truth is the firm foundation on which you must base all decisions. It is used to eliminate and discredit that which is not true and to develop relationships based on God's Truth.

You must spend time knowing God's truth by reading His Word daily before anything else.

Breastplate of Righteousness: This is Christ's Righteousness

In our response to an unjust law or in following God's commands, we must walk in accordance with what is right before

---

[157] I can recommend two great sources to learn more about this topic that I know taught me a lot. Much of these notes came from Tony Evan's *Armor of God Bible Study* and Rick Renner's book, *Dressed to Kill: A Biblical Approach to Spiritual Warfare*.

God. We must have an intentional decision to live every day pleasing to God, and it must reflect our attitudes and beliefs.

The breastplate, like the Roman soldier's armor, covers our heart and our lungs. His righteousness (be careful as it is not self-righteousness) is determined by what we breathe in and what we breathe out.

Is it hate or love?

Sarcasm or praise?

Bitterness or gratefulness?

Anger or praise?

While engaging in Christian Civil Disobedience, you need to be intentional that you are breathing in and breathing out the right attitudes and virtues.

Shoes in Preparation of Peace: This is Christ's Peace

The shoes of the soldiers had long spikes on the bottom to hold fast and stand strong when moving or when being pushed upon by your adversary.

This helps us stand strong knowing that we do not have to prove ourselves to anyone because we are His children. He is the anchor that holds us in place.

This recognition:

1. Helps prepare for persecution
2. Helps prepare us to show Godliness in a moment of adversity
3. Helps others see peace that only Jesus gives

Know that no amount of persecution can take away from knowing that you are God's child.[158] You are chosen by your almighty Father who spoke the World into existence. You are appointed by Christ to bear His fruit.[159]

Shield of Faith: This is Faith in the Gospel and its Promises

Faith is the hardest thing to have in moments of adversity. It is easy to be afraid of persecution. But when you are afraid, you need to recognize that the opposite of fear is faith (not, as we might suppose, courage). When we stand up as His ambassadors and feel so much that stands against us, we know that God chose us for this moment to advance His Kingdom.

Trust His decision when He picked you. During those frightening moments, change your language from "I am afraid" to "I don't trust God." Once you admit that the source is your lack of trust, then you can reset, repent, and state out loud, "I trust You."

We need to trust in God in all circumstances, knowing that God is sovereign. In God's sovereignty, these promises may not look the way we expect them to look, and we may not have them on this side of Heaven. However, we can have faith that:

- God will reward me

- God will protect me

- God will provide for me

- God will heal me

[158] John 1:12
[159] John 15:16, Colossians 3:12, 1 Thessalonians 1:4

Furthermore, remember the Roman shield was hooked on the side of the loin belt. This means that faith is hooked to truth.

Helmet of Salvation: This is the Assurance of Christ

Jesus died for my salvation. It is not earned through my words, my thoughts, or my deeds, but though God's grace. Although as Christians we know this, we have to remember the helmet does more than that. This allows us to have a deep compassion for others who need a Savior. Those who oppose us need a Savior, and we should have compassion for them, striving to show them what it looks like to have assurance in Christ.

As we study Christian Civil Disobedience, or any other biblical component—such as the end times, sexuality, stewardship of the earth, or even the structure of church leadership—we cannot let these things cloud the preeminence of the gospel or our understanding of who God is, who we are, and how to reconcile the two. This should always lead us to sharing the Gospel truths with those who do not know Jesus.

Sword of the Spirit: This is the Word of God

The sword is a two-sided sword. We receive the Word of God by hearing and reading, and we speak it out in response. We use it for offense and for defense. It is important to know the Bible and the heart of God so that we may always have verses at the ready to honor God and to defend the Gospel.

People will attack and ridicule you, but the Bible is perfect in its logic. Knowing God's Word and speaking it out loud is the appropriate response to persecution.

Final Thoughts:

At the end of his explanation of the armor of God, Paul finishes by saying,

> . . . praying at all times in the Spirit, with all prayer and supplication. To that end, keep alert with all perseverance, making supplication for all the saints, and also for me, that words may be given to me in opening my mouth boldly to proclaim the mystery of the gospel, for which I am an ambassador in chains, that I may declare it boldly, as I ought to speak.

Here is our call to prayer. We are to pray for the saints. We are to pray for our church leaders. And we have already seen that we are to pray for our leaders and those who persecute us. All of this is for the sake of the mystery of the Gospel.

As we pray for our authorities and as we suit up to defend ourselves against them, let us not only live in the tension of Christian Civil Disobedience, but also relish it. We must always be prepared for the world to remind us how hated we are, and we have to be ready to show love in response.

If the early Church could live in such a way that they honored God while living submissive to Nero, we can certainly take up the mantle and do the same under persecutions that have not yet reached anywhere near such a level. Of course, we can also recognize that such persecutions are only going to increase and that, in spite of that, we can still be bold. We can still pursue truth. We can still love the Lord first and be citizens reconciled to those in authority.

What Are You Willing to Give Up?

To Live, To Die

To live is Christ and to die is gain.[160] If we are to live fully for Christ, and if we are to stand firmly in opposition to policies and demands made by ruling authorities that are contradictory to our life in Christ, we have little choice but to hold to this verse.

In the end, we must be prepared for the days that the Bible tells us are coming. Evil always has and always will try to rise up against us, but as we draw nearer to that last battle, it may feel hopeless and oppressive. In that time, and as we begin to grow weary, we must hold to the verses, the prayers, and the knowledge of the goodness of God and the glory in which we will dwell after our deaths.

In addition to being prepared, we must be intentional. We have to live with a deep accordance to Scripture, letting go of the worldly distractions that try to confuse us or try to compromise our hearts.

---

[160] From Philippians 1:21

Do not look back. Like Lot's wife in the destruction of Sodom and Gomorrah[161], we may be tempted to see what there is behind us—what we are leaving, what we are running from. But our eyes should always be fixed on the work of Christ. The miserable end of the world may be fascinating, but the Gospel is a rejuvenating sight for weary eyes.

Whatever cross we are made to bear, let us bear it with the awareness that Christ is our reward.

As Christians, no matter what happens, we win.

---

[161] Genesis 19:26

Appendix A

Applying the Life of Jesus
to the Guidelines of Civil Disobedience

It is fine enough for us to discuss what we should do in the presence of evil and how we ought to stand firm, but what we have not looked at specifically is how Jesus and His disciples responded.

How can we be more like Christ? We can follow in His footsteps. Bearing each of the previous chapters in mind, we can see examples throughout Scripture of how Christ responded.

1. When do we do Civil Disobedience?
    a. When asked to do evil
        i. Jesus:
            1. During the ordered stoning of the adulteress, He refused, instead writing in the sand and telling her to go and sin no more, even as He convicted

the Pharisees who were the religious rulers
passing out judgement.

    ii.   Apostles:

        1.   In Acts 5, the Apostles were arrested
and supernaturally freed. Following
this, they returned to the temple and
began preaching. When the religious
rulers found them, they charged the
Apostles, urging them to cease in their
preaching. But they stood firm,
reminding the council of priests that,
"We must obey God rather than men."
It would have been evil if they had
stopped.

  b.   Government Law Violates God's Law

    i.   Jesus

        1.   The Sabbath day was considered a holy day, set
apart by God. So when Jesus healed a man on
that day, the religious leaders confronted Him
about disobeying one of the Ten
Commandments. Jesus, however, knew that God
had charged Him with healing and the miraculous.
This was a sign of God's wonders, and Jesus
would have been contrary to God if He had not
obeyed.

2. The Triumphal Entry of Jesus into Jerusalem on what we now celebrate as Palm Sunday was a strong statement. There are so many nuances to what Jesus did that day which do not fit into our cultural context, but He certainly made a statement to both Jews and the government under Pontius Pilate. He made a statement that donkeys were often sent by foreign governments as a message of peace. This meant that Jesus was a) a ruler in His own right and, therefore, a threat to Pilate and b) not coming to rise up against Rome, as the Jews believed the Messiah would do.

ii. Apostles

1. Returning to Acts 4-6, the Apostles did not back down from preaching the Gospel, even when it led to their arrests and threats of death. They knew that they could not back down from honoring God.

2. In Acts 10, Peter is given a vision in which he is told to eat all the foods that Jewish law expressly forbade. Just as those untouchable things were now freely available to Peter, he was called to give the Gospel to the Gentiles, that they might become children of God. Through this preaching of the Gospel, many Gentiles would come to

follow Jesus; and, as such, many of us today are children of the Father.

c. In order to follow God's commands

   i. Jesus

      1. Repeatedly, Jesus did whatever God commanded and said whatever God commanded. He never did these things on His own behalf—as we can see that "His own behalf" would have been to cower from some of these things.

      2. Peter tried to tempt Jesus to avoid the crucifixion. Jesus, however, boldly went to the cross, procuring our reconciliation with God the Father.

   ii. Apostles

      1. Acts 4 is hardly the only time Peter continued to preach after being put in jail, he did so again in Acts 12, this time along with James.

      2. Ultimately, Peter knew his death would be bad. He understood that following the laws of Christ would lead to an ugly end. Instead of backing down in the face of controversy, he stood firm in his devotion. While Peter is famous for having denied Christ three times, he is the same man Church tradition says was crucified upside down, believing himself unworthy of the same death as Jesus.

2. Basis of Civil Disobedience

   a. Rooted in fear of God and not in human anger

      i. Jesus

         1. The cleansing of the temple is a rather complicated moment in Scripture. When we look at paintings or dramatic reenactments of the scene, we do not necessarily see things as they were. Scripture tells us Jesus fashioned a whip, but this was arguably for chasing the animals out, knowing the people would follow. There is no Gospel account in which Jesus struck anyone with a whip. And turning over tables does not necessarily mean throwing them in a fury. He poured the money out, but it does not say what else he did with it. According to John 2:16, He told those selling pigeons to take them away. He was able to do all of this while still teaching. And according to Matthew 21:14, it was immediately followed by the blind and the lame coming to be healed while He was still in the temple. When this scene is used as an excuse for violent uprisings by Christians, we have to bear in mind that Jesus was not necessarily a Kevin Sorbo-like "Hercules" in this occurrence. He was simply seeking the justice of God and to purify the temple from such greed.

    ii.   Apostles

        1.   The apostles preached through the fear of God, and in Acts 2, they saw the salvation of "about three thousand souls." God continued to multiply the number of Christians through the apostles' devotion to preaching out of their love for God and fear of Him.

b.   Done for Saving Lives and not destroying them

    i.   Jesus

        1.   This is one of the primary points of the Gospel. Christ—the holy, glorious Creator of the universe in the flesh—came to die for us. He came that we might be saved.

    ii.   Apostles

        1.   This, likewise, is the whole point of why the Apostles preached—that we might know God as they knew Jesus—that through their obedience, we would become brethren.

c.   Not idolatry

    i.   Jesus

        1.   When offered kingship during the desert temptation, Jesus refused. Although still God Himself, Jesus submitted Himself to the Father.

        2.   He healed all who came to him, but He initiated with some over others on His own.

3. Jesus did not give in to temptations or value His human desires above the Father's authority.

4. When Jesus fed the 5000, they basically followed Him because they wanted more. He let them know that this was not His ministry. While it was good to feed those who were hungry, it was not *the* Gospel.

5. When Mary poured perfume over the feet of Jesus to anoint Him, Judas argued that the money ought to have been given to the poor. As Jesus told him, the poor would always be with us. Our worship of God comes before our acts and good deeds. This is why the *first* commandment is to love God. The *second* is to love others. Any "gospel" that places the poor above Christ is an idol.

6. Even Jesus would have been subject to paying taxes to Rome. The ruler of the universe—both physical and spiritual—subjected Himself to this authority.

ii. Apostles

1. The apostles did many good, kind acts of charity, but those things were only ever accompanied by the preaching of the Gospel and telling others about Jesus. They understood their priority.

2. They understood that the primary purpose of the Messiah was not to conquer the Romans, no matter how much everyone would have loved for that to happen. They knew that He came to seek and save the lost.

3. In the epistle to Philemon, Paul orders Onesimus the slave to return to his master. Instead of rooting for social justice, he roots for obedience and the example of Christians under submission.

3. Willingly Accepting Consequences

a. Jesus

i. Certainly the greatest consequence we can see Christ undergoing is the crucifixion. This had both physical implications as well as spiritual. While we are easily horrified by the physical, of greater significance was the spiritual impact as Jesus bore our sin in His body and received the weight of God's wrath against that sin. Romans 8:39 tells us that nothing can separate us from the love of God in Christ Jesus our Lord. This is because that greatest, most awful consequence in all the world has already been undertaken through the mercy and obedience of Jesus.

ii. He was attacked by the religious authorities, repeatedly. He was humiliated. He was tortured. He was driven out. He was denied. He faced every ugly aspect of humanity to remain obedient to the Father.

      iii.   Jesus was to be stoned before He managed to escape through a miracle. However, He did not back down. He never apologized nor held back to avoid consequences.

  b. Apostles

      i.   All but one apostle were willingly executed. They were jailed. They were tortured. And they did not deny Jesus at the last.

      ii.   They were attacked by the religious authorities, most likely lost people in their lives about whom they cared. They suffered discomforts, embarrassments, and more; but nothing could keep them from Jesus.

Appendix B

Works of the Holy Spirit in Acts

Pastor Allen Jackson at World Outreach Church gave an assignment that I thoroughly enjoyed doing. He asked for us to circle every time the Holy Spirit worked in the book of Acts. After I circled each incidence, I decided to categorize my list and write out where each was found.

Jesus said that when He went to heaven, he would send the Holy Spirit to us as a helper. Therefore, I think it is important to know what the Holy Spirit is capable of doing through us as believers.

Be mindful that unholy spirits can and will imitate these gifts, which is why it is critical to also know the "fruit of the Spirit" (Galatians 5:22) so you cannot be deceived by others.

Instruction:

Acts 1:2

Acts 10:20

Acts 11:12

Acts 13:2

Acts 16:6-7

Acts 20:22

Acts 22:4

Prophesy:

Acts 1:6

Acts 19:6

Acts 20:29-31

Acts 21:11

Tongues:

Acts 2:4

Acts 19:6

Encouragement:

Acts 2:14

Acts 9:20

Salvation:

Acts 2:39-41

Healing:

Acts 3:6

Acts 8:7

Acts 8:13

Acts 8:15

Acts 9:17-18

Acts 9:20

Acts 9:34

Acts 14:11-12

Acts 28:8

Words of Wisdom:

Acts 4:8

Acts 6:10

Acts 8:29

Acts 20:29

Judgment:

Acts 5:3

Acts 5:10

Acts 13:9-11

Acts 19:21

Witness:

Acts 5:32

Evangelism:

    Acts 6:37

    Acts 8:39

    Acts 10:45

    Acts 18:5

Comfort:

    Acts 7:55

    Acts 9:31

Resurrection:

    Acts 9:40

    Acts 20:10

Words of Knowledge:

    Acts 10:19

    Acts 11:28

    Acts 19:21

    Acts 20:23

Deliverance:

    Acts 16:8

Raises Leaders:

    Acts 20:28

Faith:

Acts 27:23-28

Appendix C

Christian Warning about LGBT Issues

One of the groups that seems to get Christians caught up in emotions is the LGBT community. There are generally three kinds of Christians: those who try to defend the behavior, those who try to condemn the behavior, and those who try to ignore it.

Engaging in Civil Disobedience does not mean that you are engaging against a person. But Civil Disobedience *can* include not engaging in a behavior that is required by a civil authority.

Our job as Christians is not to judge those who are same-sex attracted just as it is not our job to judge those who lust after the opposite sex. I do not want anyone to take the words of this book as a reason to attack those who are living a lifestyle that we feel is contrary to the nature of God.

The gospel message really starts in Genesis when God says, "Let us make man in our image . . . " So the message isn't, *what sexual identity do I identify with?* but rather, *how can we be transformed into the likeness of a Holy God?*

We are not trying to transform God into the image of us (whether as a homosexual or a heterosexual). Rather, we need to follow His plan for us to become like Jesus.

Sexually, we have two choices. We can live a single life of sexual abstinence, or we can live a faithful, committed life to our married partner (in this context I mean "marriage" as defined in biblical terms, not legal terms).

Instead of judging others or enabling them, we ought to be showing them a much better alternative, which is Christ Jesus. We can let the Holy Spirit sort them out. I am thankful that my personal sexual sins were not an inhibitor against my coming to know Jesus. He loved me in spite of my sins—so much that He died for them.

However, we must still try to live a life that is holy, and we cannot do so if we actively and without apology live in sin.

The best example of a person who transformed from sexual sin, but did not fully accept Christ, was Larry Flynt. Flynt was famous for publishing *Hustler,* a uniquely graphic adult magazine. Early in 1977 he was brought to trial on obscenity and pornography charges. It resulted in a lengthy court battle, his name being whispered around water coolers and dinner tables.

Even bigger news came toward the end of that year when Larry Flynt started calling himself a Christian, with some well-known Christians backing up his story. He shared his conversion story with the Washington Post.

Dusk was falling when the Lear jet left the Ohio airport and the Lord began talking to Larry Flynt. With Ruth Carter Stapleton [the sister of President Carter, well known for her faith] seated nearby, Flynt fell to his knees, his thick hands clasped in prayer as the jet headed for the West Coast.

The feeling began as a warm, tingling, powerful sensation. Flynt could feel a slightly medicinal taste rising from his throat. He was frightened but outwardly calm as the vision appeared: a man laughing heartily and calling himself Paul stood with Jesus Christ.

"I promised to give up my wife for Him," Flynt said. "I promised to see myself castrated, to look down and see myself with no sexual organs and look up and say, 'Yes, God, it's okay, if that's Your will, that's fine.' I spoke in tongues. There were animals eating at my neck, like baboons and monkeys, gnawing at me. He told me my calling: to bring peace on earth. And He told me there had been a distortion of His Word, which confirmed my thing on religions but only one God."[162]

I hope you, like me, have some alarm bells ringing at this point. Yes, apart from the fact that this is a pretty freaky "vision," he then

---

[162] Maxa, R., A staff writer for the Magazine, & Has covered Larry Flynt's adventures for more than a year. (1978, January 08). Hustling for the lord. Retrieved April 12, 2021, from https://www.washingtonpost.com/archive/lifestyle/magazine/1978/01/08/hustling-for-the-lord/ace7c1f8-650c-4ce4-8022-223bddbd2e42/

claimed, "And He told me there had been a distortion of His Word." You know that this is not coming from God. If anything, it is too similar to the story Joseph Smith told when he founded Mormonism. Or Mohammed when he founded Islam.[163]

Larry's story continues in the Post:

> It is evening, two weeks before Christmas, and the founder of Hustler magazine has decked the halls of his Columbus mansion with boughs of holly. Dozens of poinsettias and holiday floral arrangements fill his Tudor home. Outside, a grand fir tree is hung with oversized candy canes and lights that are reflected softly in a blanket of snow. Inside, Larry Flynt is rearranging his life according to the dictates of God. . . .
>
> Flynt tells his staffers he intends to consult with sex education and religion experts in New York about Christian ways to present nudity.
>
> "There will be a rabbi there and a . . . what's that religion that starts with an 'E'?"
>
> "Episcopalian," someone volunteers.
>
> ". . . right, an Episcopalian priest. But I don't want you to think I'm going to sit down with biblical scholars and let them run the magazine. I'll use them for

---

[163] For a great account of Mohammad's story and the flawed religious experience, read *Seeking Allah, Finding Jesus* by Nabeel Qureshi

reference. If I have any questions, I'll just fall right down on my knees and ask Him [God] what to do."

"To begin with, says Flynt, there will be no more photo spreads of women by themselves - sex must be presented in a "natural, healthy way" with a man included in the feature."

Larry Flynt, who built his kingdom publishing pornography was trying to find ways to make it fit into his version of "Christianity."

Outwardly he confessed, "Jesus is Lord," but inwardly he was redefining what that meant to suit himself. He was attempting to create God in his image rather than allowing himself to be transformed into the likeness of a Holy God.

The article printed above was published in January 1978. A few months later, Flynt was shot by a sniper outside the courthouse in Lawrenceville, Georgia, where he stood trial. The shot didn't kill him, but it left him paralyzed from the waist down. It was at this point that instead of turning to the God he claimed to know, he turned away. He proclaimed himself an atheist once again. The last years of his life were spent in seclusion—rarely leaving his house and surrounding himself with heavily armed bodyguards. He lived in fear and died without any evidence of true repentance.

Flynt confessed "sin," but would pick and choose what he would truly turn from and what he would embrace. He tried to whitewash sinful interests by gaining approval from religious figures. He adopted a form of godliness but didn't allow the power of God to transform him through the renewing of his mind. He praised a caricature of God rather than God Himself.

If we can look at God's Word in all its fullness, without defensiveness and pride, we have a chance to truly let the Holy Spirit teach us His truth. This translates to our understanding of Salvation as well. It's perhaps time for the Church to let go of some of its hardline stances or preferences and willingly look at the Bible (in its entirety) so that God has room to reveal His truth to our hearts and minds **based on His Word**.

The purpose of the gospel is not to get into heaven but to be transformed into the image of a holy God. Transformation is a process, and we are never fully transformed until we die.

This is the warning I am giving:

1. Do not attack people who are LGBT and condemn them for wrongdoing as you walk about in your own sinful body. Point to what God says.

2. Do not pervert God's truth in a way that enables others to walk in their own sinful body. Again: Point to what God says.

Civil Disobedience may require us to stand for God's truth in the face of societal demands that conflict with our faith, but it does not require us to force our ideas on those who don't know Jesus.

Appendix D

Business and Civil Disobedience

In Burwell v Hobby Lobby, 573 U.S. 682 (2014), the US Supreme Court recognized that a closely held corporation can have a religious belief. As a result, business owners and closely held corporations must recognize that the business can also engage in Christian Civil Disobedience.

Businesses are restricted in what they can and cannot do as they cannot be discriminatory in nature. But, just like individuals, any business that would engage in discrimination in the name of Christianity is not Christian. They cannot play favorites for promotions or favor based on their religious beliefs.

However, what happens when the business is required to do an evil act by following the law? Would the business then be disobedient to God?

Hobby Lobby is a great example of this. When the Affordable Care Act was passed, there was a provision that required businesses to provide coverage for contraceptives, including some options which Hobby Lobby felt amounted to abortion due to the nature of how those contraceptives worked not only to prevent but to end a pregnancy.

Although they took their fight through the legal system, Hobby Lobby was prepared to close their stores if they lost the fight and continued to defy the mandate, potentially amassing millions of dollars in fines per day.

Their motivation, rooted in the fear of God, was to save lives and not destroy them. They did not attack businesses that supported the mandate, nor did they try to destroy others because they could not get their way.

Yet, like individuals who engage in Civil Disobedience, Hobby Lobby recognized they could close, which for a business is essentially jail time or execution. They were criticized by Christian and non-Christian groups alike. In other words, they accepted and suffered the consequences for these actions.

There have been countless other examples where businesses refused to cater a LGBT wedding and were forced to close under protests and boycotts.

Christian business owners must recognize that our theology is not based on one's prosperity, bottom-line, or happiness. Like all Christians, our story is made complete during our trials and our sufferings.

Similarly, a Christian employee can be asked to not pray or talk about Jesus in the workplace or on their lunch break. Should an employee engage in Civil Disobedience against the corporate world for which they work? Absolutely! But recognize this: Your actions at work are not entitled, and there will be consequences for your actions. You could be terminated, forced to quit, or ostracized.

There are many people who have faced this circumstance, and they all are handling it differently.

A husband of a friend of mine works for a large corporation. For him to pray out loud would cause others to be upset, and he would be terminated. He is choosing to stay to keep the benefits he has amassed working there.

Another friend of mine, who works for a regional business, has been told that he is no longer allowed to pray at work; and he is quitting his job after he finds another place to work.

I had someone reach out to me to tell me they were called into their boss's office at a small, family-run business because of a complaint that she was praying in her cubicle in the mornings. She has decided to continue to pray quietly so no one is able to hear her.

Lastly, Joe Kennedy, a football coach was fired for refusing to stop a silent prayer after each game.

There is nothing wrong with what each of these people have decided to do, provided that they asked God first what their approach needed to be. There is not a right or wrong answer, but know that if you choose to engage in Civil Disobedience with your boss, you will (and you should) suffer the consequences for it.

Whatever your convictions, let the words of Matthew 6:33 lead you to "seek first the kingdom of God and His righteousness."

About the Author

When Peter Demos met Christ late in life, he turned his business over to God, acknowledging that he is only a steward of God's business. Peter believes that all business should be used to follow Christ's commission, which is to share the Gospel and equip disciples.

As president and attorney for Demos Brands, Peter Demos has been in business leadership for decades. He is a highly sought-after speaker who inspires others of all walks of life to lead with courage and purpose. He uses his failures and successes as teaching opportunities to encourage others to grow. Peter regularly speaks to organizations on faith, business, and personal growth.

Peter has been interviewed on dozens of podcasts, radio, and tv shows and has written many articles about applying Christian principles to current events.

Peter's first book, *Afraid to Trust*, details his journey to Christ, applying Biblical principles to a failed business.

To learn more about Peter or to request him to speak to your group, please visit www.PeterDemos.org.